I0503865

Table des matières

Introduction

In recent years, the world has witnessed a significant transformation in the way we work, with remote work emerging as the new norm for countless professionals globally. While working from home offers unparalleled flexibility and autonomy, it also presents unique challenges, such as maintaining a healthy work-life balance and staying productive amidst isolation. If you've ever found yourself grappling with these challenges, rest assured that there's a better approach to remote work, one that enables you to lead a balanced, fulfilling life while excelling in your career.

This book is your detailed guide to achieving exactly that. We've compiled an extensive array of practical tips, strategies, and exercises tailored to help you create a successful and satisfying remote work experience that caters to your unique needs and goals. By following the advice in this book, you'll learn how to design an inspiring home workspace, establish routines and habits that promote productivity and well-being, and nurture mental and emotional health.

Furthermore, this book will provide you with the tools and insights needed to take control of your career growth and development. Through personal growth planning, virtual networking strategies, and goal-setting exercises, you'll be empowered to thrive professionally and unlock your full potential in your remote career.

Picture a work-from-home life where you feel energized, focused, and in control, where you can strike a healthy balance between your personal and professional life while reaping the benefits of remote work. By implementing the advice and practices outlined in this book, you'll be well on your way to making that vision a reality.

Set off on a transformative trip that will forever alter your approach to remote work. You can build a work-from-home existence that supports balance, success, and wellbeing, propelling you towards a brighter future in your profession and beyond, with the appropriate mentality, techniques, and commitment.

Take advantage of this book's invaluable insights to change your remote work experience. Discover the methods that will allow you to live a healthy, balanced lifestyle while increasing your productivity and professional progress. Learn how to organize your home office, include physical activity into your daily routine, practice mindfulness, and form meaningful social connections.

As you progress through each chapter, you'll be equipped with practical exercises that will encourage you to apply the knowledge and strategies shared, ultimately leading to tangible improvements in your remote work life. From assessing your current routine and creating a personal growth plan to setting fitness goals and evaluating your eating habits, these exercises will provide a roadmap for continuous growth and self-improvement.

In an increasingly digital and interconnected world, mastering the art of remote work is essential for long-term career success. Don't let the challenges of remote work hold you back. Instead, harness its potential by embracing the strategies and techniques shared within these pages. By doing so, you'll not only enhance your well-being and productivity, but you'll also create a work-from-home life that is both personally and professionally fulfilling.

Now is the time to take control of your remote work journey and transform it into an empowering and rewarding experience. Let this book be your guide as you embark on a path towards balance, success, and wellness in your remote career. The future of work is here, and with the right approach, you can seize its limitless potential.

Section 1

Laying the Foundation

Chapter 1: The Remote Work Revolution

Embracing the New World of Work

Understanding the benefits and challenges of remote work

Remote work has ushered in a new era of autonomy and independence for professionals all around the world. As more individuals choose this method of working, it's critical to grasp the advantages and disadvantages of remote work. This section will offer a review of the benefits and drawbacks of remote work, as well as techniques for overcoming various hurdles.

The advantages of remote work:

1. Increased flexibility: remote work allows you to design a schedule that is tailored to your own requirements and preferences, resulting in a better work-life balance. You can more easily handle personal commitments, appointments, and family time if you have the option to determine your work

hours. Better flexibility can lead to better job satisfaction and well-being.

2. Working from home eliminates the need to commute to an office, saving you time, money, and worry. The time and energy saved by not commuting can be spent on more constructive activities such as exercise, hobbies, or spending time with family and friends. Furthermore, cutting commuting times benefits the environment by minimizing carbon emissions from transportation.

3. Workplace customization: when working remotely, you may create a workplace that is personalized to your preferences, which can boost productivity and comfort. Personalizing your work environment, whether by choosing the proper lighting, installing ergonomic furniture, or surrounding oneself with inspiring design, may lead to enhanced motivation and job satisfaction.

4. Cost savings: working from home typically results in cost savings because you no longer need to spend money on commute, professional dress, or meals away from home. These savings can be utilized to improve your quality of life by investing in your home office or other personal objectives.

The difficulties of remote work:

1. Isolation: because remote work can be isolating, it is critical to maintain social relationships and overcome emotions of loneliness. Consider joining online forums or interest groups,

attending virtual networking events, or organizing frequent video conversations with colleagues and friends to address this problem. You may lessen the consequences of isolation and maintain a strong support network by actively pursuing social contacts.

2. Distractions: working from home can bring a plethora of distractions, necessitating discipline and attention in order to be effective. Create a specific workspace that is free of interruptions and noise to reduce distractions. Setting limits with family members and pets, as well as establishing a daily routine, may help you keep focused and on track.

3. Keeping a good work-life balance: with the borders between work and personal life becoming increasingly blurred, it is critical to create boundaries in order to avoid burnout and retain well-being. Establish a consistent work schedule and be sure to take breaks and detach from work during your downtime. Self-care activities such as exercise, meditation, or hobby pursuits can also help you maintain a balanced lifestyle.

4. Communication issues: because remote work frequently relies on virtual communication, misunderstandings or misinterpretations might occur. To overcome this obstacle, practice clear and concise communication, use many communication methods (e.g., email, instant messaging, or

video conferences), and check in with colleagues on a frequent basis to ensure everyone is on the same page.

To summarize, remote work has various advantages, including improved flexibility, shorter commuting times, a more customized work environment, and cost savings. It does, however, create obstacles such as solitude, diversions, achieving a healthy work-life balance, and communication difficulties. By recognizing these advantages and disadvantages, you may devise ways to overcome any roadblocks and leverage the benefits of remote work, resulting in a more successful and rewarding job.

Identifying the skills needed to thrive in a remote environment.

Working from home has become more common in today's quickly changing work world. To succeed in a remote work environment, it is critical to develop and reinforce key abilities and attributes. This section will go into the key talents required for successful remote work and provide advice on how to enhance these abilities.

1. Self-discipline: remote work necessitates self-motivation and the ability to stay focused in the absence of regular monitoring. It is critical to establish a daily schedule that includes designated work hours and regular breaks in order to cultivate self-discipline. Setting clear boundaries between

work and personal life is also essential for avoiding burnout and maintaining productivity. Setting reasonable objectives and evaluating progress can also provide motivation and a sense of accomplishment, encouraging self-control.

2. Time management: effective time management is critical for productivity and achieving a healthy work-life balance. Consider using time management techniques such as the Pomodoro Technique, time blocking, or the two-minute rule to improve your time management skills. These approaches can assist you in allocating time and prioritizing work more successfully. Using productivity tools such as calendars, to-do lists, and project management software can also help you keep organized and on schedule.

3. Clear and straightforward communication is essential when working remotely, as misconceptions are more likely in a virtual context. Practice active listening and make sure you completely understand your team members' opinions before replying to improve your communication abilities. Furthermore, depending on the complexity and urgency of the situation, use suitable communication channels (e.g., email, instant messaging, or video calls). Consider doing regular check-ins and feedback meetings with your team to encourage open communication and to resolve any problems or misconceptions as soon as possible.

4. Adaptability: dealing with unanticipated obstacles or changing conditions is common in remote employment. It is critical to be able to adapt fast and come up with inventive solutions in order to thrive in a distant situation. Focus on having a growth mindset, which entails viewing problems as opportunities for learning and progress, to increase adaptability. Accept change and seek out new experiences that will take you beyond of your comfort zone. You'll grow more robust and more ready to deal with any challenges that remote work may provide.

5. Collaboration: even if you work remotely, teamwork is still an important element of most jobs. Make a concerted effort to engage with your coworkers and participate in team activities to improve your cooperation skills. To maintain open communication and stay connected with your team, use collaborative solutions such as shared documents, project management systems, and video conferencing. Furthermore, being proactive in offering support and assistance to your coworkers builds a healthy and collaborative work environment.

6. Technical abilities: remote work frequently necessitates the use of numerous technologies and tools to execute tasks and stay in touch with colleagues. It is critical to become acquainted with relevant software, applications, and communication platforms in order to flourish in a remote

context. Maintain your technical abilities and remain up to date on new tools that can improve your remote work experience.

7. Emotional intelligence: working remotely can cause feelings of isolation or separation from your team. Developing emotional intelligence - the capacity to perceive, comprehend, and control your own emotions as well as the emotions of others – can assist you in navigating the emotional obstacles of remote work. During virtual discussions, practice empathy and be mindful of your colleagues' emotional indicators. You will be more suited to develop solid relationships and maintain a friendly remote work environment if you cultivate emotional intelligence.

Finally, thriving in a remote work environment necessitates the development and refinement of numerous abilities and attributes. You'll be well-prepared to succeed in your remote work environment and achieve career success if you focus on self-discipline, time management, effective communication, adaptability, teamwork, technical abilities, and emotional intelligence.

Tips for transitioning smoothly to remote work.

Because of the COVID-19 pandemic, many of us have had to adapt swiftly to remote work, frequently without much preparation or direction. As time goes on, some companies have adopted a hybrid approach that combines remote and in-person employment, while others have made remote work a permanent choice. Excelling at remote work can be difficult, especially for people who are used to the structure and social components of typical office settings.

In this section, we'll present practical advice and tactics for ensuring a smooth and lasting shift to remote work, considering the changes caused by the epidemic and the changing nature of work. You'll be able to minimize the challenges of remote work and create a supportive environment that fosters productivity and well-being in the long run by covering topics like setting up a dedicated workspace, establishing routines, and leveraging technology to stay connected with colleagues and clients.

As we navigate this new normal, we must keep in mind that our experiences and needs may shift over time. Maintaining your performance and well-being in a remote or hybrid work environment will need a focus on adaptability, resilience, and ongoing improvement. You can ensure that you not only survive but prosper in this new era of work if you have the correct strategies in place.

1. Set up a dedicated workspace

Having a dedicated workspace is essential for maintaining focus and productivity when working remotely. To create an effective workspace:

- Choose a quiet, comfortable location with minimal distractions.
- Ensure proper lighting and ergonomic furniture to prevent eye strain and physical discomfort.
- Keep your workspace organized and clutter-free to promote a clear mind and efficient work habits.
- Personalize your space with items that inspire and motivate you, such as plants, artwork, or motivational quotes.

2. Establish routines and boundaries

Developing routines and setting boundaries can help you maintain a healthy work-life balance while working from home. To establish effective routines and boundaries:

- Create a consistent schedule, setting specific work hours and breaks throughout the day.
- Establish a morning routine to signal the start of your workday and an end-of-work routine to help you disconnect.
- Communicate your work schedule and boundaries to family members, roommates, or anyone else sharing your living space.
- Prioritize self-care, ensuring you make time for regular exercise, healthy meals, and relaxation.

3. Leverage technology to stay connected

Staying connected with colleagues and clients is crucial for remote workers. To effectively leverage technology for communication and collaboration:

- Familiarize yourself with video conferencing, instant messaging, and project management tools.
- Establish guidelines and best practices for using these tools within your team to ensure clear and efficient communication.
- Schedule regular virtual meetings and check-ins with colleagues and supervisors to maintain strong working relationships.
- Be mindful of your online presence, ensuring you remain professional and engaged during virtual meetings and interactions.

4. Set clear goals and prioritize tasks

When working remotely, it's essential to set clear goals and prioritize tasks to stay focused and motivated. To effectively manage your workload:

- Break down long-term goals into smaller, achievable milestones.
- Create a daily to-do list, prioritizing tasks based on deadlines and importance.
- Use productivity techniques, such as time blocking or the Eisenhower Matrix, to allocate your time and energy effectively.

- Regularly review your progress and adjust your priorities as needed.

5. Stay proactive and accountable

Without the immediate presence of supervisors and colleagues, remote workers need to take greater responsibility for their own progress and productivity. To stay proactive and accountable:

- Communicate regularly with your team, providing updates on your work and any challenges you're facing.
- Seek feedback and guidance from colleagues and supervisors to ensure you're on the right track.
- Set personal performance targets and track your progress towards achieving them.
- Develop a growth mindset, viewing setbacks and challenges as opportunities for learning and improvement.

6. Maintain a strong work-life balance

It can be challenging to separate work and personal life when working from home. To maintain a strong work-life balance:

- Establish boundaries between work and personal time, resisting the temptation to work outside of your designated hours.
- Make time for hobbies, socializing, and relaxation to recharge and maintain your well-being.
- Set limits on work-related technology use during personal time, such as checking emails or taking work calls.

- Develop strategies for managing stress and maintaining resilience in the face of work-related challenges.

In conclusion, transitioning smoothly to remote work involves creating a dedicated workspace, establishing routines and boundaries, leveraging technology, setting clear goals, staying proactive and accountable, and maintaining a strong work-life balance. By following these practical tips and strategies, you'll be able to minimize the challenges associated with remote work and create a supportive environment that fosters productivity, well-being, and success in your career.

The following chapters will dive deeper into these topics, providing thorough guidance, expert views, and actionable solutions for each one of them. By delving into these areas, you will obtain a good grasp of how to optimize your remote work experience and establish a lasting, meaningful work-life balance that contributes to your overall success and happiness.

Embark in this journey and take advantage of the great chances that remote work provides. You may prosper in your remote career while also living a healthier, more balanced lifestyle if you have the correct techniques in place and a dedication to continual growth.

Chapter 2: Designing Your Ideal Home Workspace

Ergonomics, Functionality, and Inspiration

Choosing the right location and setting up your workspace

Having a positive and fruitful experience when working from home starts with making smart decisions about where to set up shop and how to organize your workspace. When choosing a site for your home office, you should take into consideration the following factors:

1. Choose a location that is somewhat quiet and free of any interruptions or disturbances. If you live with other people, such as relatives or roommates, you should look for a room that has a door that can be closed in order to have more privacy and lessen the amount of noise. If you don't have access to a separate room, one option for minimizing distractions is to use headphones with active noise cancellation or a machine that generates white noise.

2. Natural light: studies have shown that being exposed to natural light may have a positive effect on one's mood, level of alertness, and overall productivity. If possible, pick a location that has windows or is in close proximity to a natural light source. Alternatively, if you want to create an environment that is cozy and well-lit, you may make an investment in high-quality artificial lighting that imitates natural light.

3. Essentials for the space: think about how much space you'll need for office equipment such as a desk, chair, computer, and storage space. Ensure that there is sufficient room to suit your requirements without making you feel crowded or overwhelmed.

4. Power outlets and an internet connection: the power outlets and internet connection at your workstation should be simple to access so that you can charge your electronic devices, and the internet connection should be strong and reliable so that you may participate in video chats and complete other online responsibilities.

After you have selected the most suitable location for your home office, you should concentrate on arranging your workspace in accordance with the following recommendations:

1. Invest in a high-quality workstation and seat for yourself: it is essential for both productivity and well-being to have a desk that is well-designed and ergonomic. Pick a workstation that

has sufficient room for working, as well as a chair that provides sufficient lumbar support, can be adjusted in height, and has armrests.

2. Organize your workspace: make use of several kinds of storage, such as shelves, drawers, and file cabinets, in order to keep the appearance of your working area neat and tidy. To minimize the amount of disruption caused by your activity, always keep items that are often needed within easy reach.

3. Make advantage of several options for cable management: wires and cables should be kept neat and organized in order to maintain a clean and professional appearance at your workspace. To prevent the cables from becoming tangled or causing a trip hazard, it is best to bundle them together using cable ties or clips.

4. Put your personal stamp on the area: personalize your workspace by adding pictures, artwork, or plants to create an environment that is engaging and stimulating for you to be in. These qualities have the potential to make you feel more at ease and comfortable, both of which can lead to an increase in your output.

If you choose your office's location with care and consider its layout, you may produce an environment that is pleasurable, functional, and inspirational, which in turn encourages productivity and well-being.

Ensuring proper ergonomics for comfort and productivity

Ergonomics play a crucial role in maintaining comfort and preventing work-related injuries, such as musculoskeletal disorders, repetitive strain injuries, and eye strain. To ensure proper ergonomics in your home office, follow these guidelines:

1. Chair positioning: choose a chair with adjustable height, lumbar support, and armrests. Adjust the chair so that your feet are flat on the ground, your knees are at a 90-degree angle, and your hips are slightly higher than your knees. Ensure that the backrest supports the natural curve of your spine, and adjust the armrests to support your forearms when typing.

2. Desk height: your desk should be at a height that allows you to maintain a comfortable posture with your shoulders relaxed and your elbows at a 90-degree angle when typing. If possible, consider investing in a height-adjustable desk that allows you to switch between sitting and standing throughout the day.

3. Monitor placement: position your monitor at an arm's length away, with the top of the screen at eye level or slightly below. This placement helps reduce eye strain and encourages proper

posture. If you use multiple monitors, position them close together to minimize head and neck movement.

4. Keyboard and mouse placement: the placement of your keyboard and mouse is critical for maintaining proper posture and preventing strain on your wrists, arms, and shoulders. Follow these guidelines for optimal keyboard and mouse positioning:

• Position the keyboard directly in front of you, with the keys at a comfortable height that allows your arms to maintain a 90-degree angle when typing. Ensure that your wrists are in a neutral position, neither flexed nor extended, and that your shoulders are relaxed.

• Place the mouse next to the keyboard, within easy reach, and at the same level as the keyboard to minimize the need for extended reaching or awkward wrist movements. Consider using an ergonomic mouse designed to reduce strain on the wrist and forearm.

• Use a wrist rest or a gel pad to provide support for your wrists when typing or using the mouse. This support can help reduce pressure on the wrists and minimize the risk of repetitive strain injuries.

• Take frequent breaks to stretch your arms, wrists, and shoulders. Regular movement can help prevent stiffness and discomfort associated with prolonged periods of typing and mouse use.

Personalizing your space for inspiration and motivation

It's possible that giving your workplace some personal touch and inspiration will have a significant impact on your motivation, productivity, and overall well-being. When it comes to personalizing your home office, take into consideration the following ideas:

1. Include your preferred colors: choose a color scheme that best reflects your character and aesthetic preferences. You may inject color into a space by using paint, hanging artwork on the walls, or incorporating decorative items such as pillows, rugs, or other office accessories.

2. Exhibit personal things such as: surround yourself with things that are important to you or that bring back joyful memories, such as pictures of your family, keepsakes from trips you've taken, or pieces of artwork. While you are working, these things might serve as a source of inspiration and motivation for you.

3. Bring the outside in by bringing plants into your workspace, which may assist to improve air quality, reduce stress, and create a workplace that is more aesthetically pleasing. The pothos, the snake plant, and the spider plant are all examples of low-maintenance houseplants that thrive well in a variety of environments.

4. In order to act as a constant reminder of your purpose and aims, you should post motivational words, affirmations, or goals in visible places across your workplace.

For home office workers with limited space or shared environments

The following points offer practical solutions to make the most of your situation:

1. When you are working with a restricted amount of square footage, you should make advantage of the vertical space by installing shelves, wall-mounted workstations, or hanging storage options. If you use this strategy, it might help you make the most of your workspace while also keeping it tidy and decluttering it at the same time.

2. Construct areas that can serve several purposes. If you and your family or roommates share a workspace, you might want to give some thought to building an area that can do several different tasks. Include in your setup either a table that can be folded up or transformed into a dining table when it is not being used for work-related activities.

3. Install room dividers to create an atmosphere of privacy and seclusion in your home office, even if it is in a common space. If you want to maintain focus during work hours, you might want to consider partitioning the space with bookshelves, folding screens, or drapes.

4. Build boundaries and establish routines: when working in a shared workplace with other members of your family, it is essential to create boundaries and establish routines with each other. Make sure your work hours and expectations are clear to everyone and think about using visual cues like a "Do Not Disturb" sign to let others know when you need uninterrupted work time.

5. Invest in a set of headphones with active noise cancellation if you want to limit the amount of time lost to distractions brought on by background noise. Even if your office is chaotic and noisy, you will be able to maintain your concentration and get a lot of work done thanks to this strategy.

6. If you don't have a dedicated workplace, you may still make your office seem more like your own by adding easily transportable items like a lap desk, desk organizers, or a lumbar support cushion to your workspace. This enables you to quickly create and disassemble your desk as required, all while maintaining a feeling of uniqueness and comfort in the process.

By making changes to the way your home office looks and functions, you can transform it into an engaging setting that is conducive to your productivity while you are working from home. Putting in the effort to design a workspace that caters to your own preferences can not only lead to an increase in your overall productivity, but it will also help to make your time at work more enjoyable and satisfying.

Practice: create a workspace checklist and evaluate your current setup

Build a workspace checklist and evaluate the way things are currently arranged. To guarantee that your home office fits your requirements and inspires productivity on your part, you should develop a workspace checklist that outlines the primary elements that comprise your ideal working environment. When developing your own checklist, be sure to keep the following sections in mind:

1. Ergonomics: assessing your current setup for your desk, chair, monitor, keyboard, and mouse will help you identify areas that might be improved. Adjust or purchase ergonomic tools to reduce discomfort and protect yourself from injuries that may be caused by your job.

2. Structure: Examine the possibilities for organizing and storage that are present in your workspace. Locate any disorganization or clutter in your workstation that could be preventing you from being productive, and then use strategies to improve its overall structure.

3. Illumination: examine the levels of natural and artificial illumination in your workplace to ascertain whether it satisfies your requirements. If you want to increase the lighting in your

workstation, you might want to think about installing additional light sources or modifying the window coverings.

4. Personalization: take into consideration the amount of personalization that is already present in your workspace and look for places where you might add some personal touches or find some inspiration. This might be accomplished by incorporating works of art, plants, or other decorative accents that are reflective of your individuality and aesthetic preferences.

Check out how things are currently set up at your home office with the help of your workspace checklist, then make any necessary adjustments. Making sure that your requirements and preferences are met at your office may help you create an environment that is beneficial to both your productivity and your overall health and well-being.

Section 2

Building Healthy Routines

Chapter 3: Establishing a Balanced Work-Life Integration

Time Management and Prioritization

Setting a consistent schedule and routine

When working from home or another location and maintaining a regular routine is essential. Maintaining your focus, effectively managing your time, and striking a good balance between your job and personal life may all be aided by a routine that is well-structured. In the following paragraphs, we will discuss the steps necessary to create a daily schedule that not only balances one's professional and personal responsibilities but also prioritizes one's productivity and sense of well-being.

1. Create a consistent routine by beginning with establishing regular work hours, which is one of the first steps in the process of building a consistent routine. Find out when you are at your most productive and then structure your workweek around those times. It is possible that adhering to a standard nine to five work schedule or taking a more flexible approach, such as working early in the morning and late in the evening

with a break in the middle of the day, will be necessary. Explaining your work schedule to your coworkers and clients can help you create clear expectations for them.

2. Include breaks: breaks are essential for preventing burnout and maintaining focus, so be sure to include them. Make it a point to give yourself regular breaks to stretch, relax, and reenergize throughout the day. It is possible that there may be breaks of fifteen minutes in the morning and afternoon, in addition to a lengthier break for lunch. Make the most of these pauses by partaking in activities that will help you relax, such as going for a walk, practicing mindfulness, or connecting with friends or family.

3. Establish a morning routine: it has been shown that having a regular morning routine may assist set the stage for a productive day at work. To help you transition from your personal life to your work life, devise a series of activities that you can do, such as going for a run, practicing meditation, or writing. It's possible that this practice will assist you in mentally preparing for the day ahead and helping you establish a distinct boundary between your personal and professional life.

4. Make a schedule for your typical activities: create a list of the tasks that need to be completed before beginning each new workday. Put these activities in order of importance, depending on the due dates, and then schedule adequate time

for each one of them. This can help you become more organized and keep your attention on the most crucial aspects of your professional responsibilities.

5. Spend some time focusing on yourself and the things that interest you most: it is essential to maintain a healthy balance between one's personal life and one's professional life, even when working from home. Include in your daily schedule things that promote good self-care, such as physical activity, meditation, and hobbies you like doing. This can be of assistance to you in the management of stress, the maintenance of your mental and physical well-being, and the prevention of burnout.

6. Review and adjust your schedule. It is important to review and make adjustments to your schedule on a frequent basis to ensure that it continues to be productive and is in line with both your personal and professional objectives. Changes in your working hours, reevaluation of your priorities, or the introduction of fresh methods of self-care might all fall under this category.

When you work from home, having a routine and a set strategy may help you stay focused, be more productive with your time, and strike a better balance between your job and your personal life. Develop a daily routine that is beneficial to your productivity and well-being by deciding on regular work hours, scheduling breaks, and allocating time for self-care and personal interests.

Techniques for task prioritization and time management

When you are working from home, it is essential to have strong time management skills in order to effectively manage your tasks and maintain your productivity. In this section, we will provide you with actionable guidance for prioritizing activities, setting goals, and managing your time in order to assist you in remaining on track with the commitments associated to your place of employment. We will discuss a variety of methods for managing time, such as the Eisenhower Matrix, the Pomodoro Technique, and time blocking, with the goal of assisting readers in selecting the method that is most suitable for them.

1. The Eisenhower Matrix is an easy method for categorizing different tasks according to their level of importance and the amount of time they need. There are four different kinds of tasks: those that are urgent and important, those that are important but not urgent, those that are urgent but not important, and those that are neither urgent nor important. You will be able to concentrate on what is truly essential if you organize your responsibilities following such typology,

while also avoiding being overwhelmed by jobs that are not as vital.

The Eisenhower Decision Matrix

https://luxafor.com/the-eisenhower-matrix/

2. The Pomodoro Technique is a method of time management that involves breaking up your work into short, focused intervals (usually 25 minutes each), which are referred to as "pomodoros," and then taking a short break in between each pomodoro. After you have completed four pomodoros, you should relax for a longer period of time. This method can help improve focus, minimize fatigue, and make it easier to complete major tasks by breaking down large activities into smaller, more manageable chunks.

3. The process of allocating specific chunks of time on your calendar to particular activities or categories of work is

referred to as "time blocking." You may, for instance, arrange two hours of focused work in the morning, one hour of meetings in the afternoon, and then another hour of administrative work in the evening. Time blocking is a technique that can assist you in staying organized, maintaining your concentration, and devoting sufficient time to your most important activities.

4. At work, maintaining your concentration and staying motivated will be much easier if you set goals that are specific, measurable, achievable, relevant, and time-bound (SMART). Your efforts will have a clearly defined direction if you use these objectives, and it will be simple to monitor how well you are doing. To ensure that you are held responsible, break down more ambitious objectives into more manageable steps and evaluate your progress on a consistent basis.

5. Make a list of everything you need to get done before you start your workday, and then arrange the items on the list in order of importance and the amount of time you have available to complete each one. First tackle the most important errands, and then continue working your way down the list. Using this strategy might make it easier for you to maintain organization and channel your time and effort into the pursuits that are most meaningful to you.

6. Getting rid of distractions. Distractions can have a significant negative impact on productivity and make it more challenging to effectively manage one's time. Find the sources of distraction that are most common in your home office and take steps to reduce their impact, such as social media, email notifications, and ambient noise. It may be helpful in this regard to install internet filters, set specific times for checking email, or work in an office that is kept relatively quiet.

7. Maintaining and improving your abilities in time management through frequent review and training: it is essential to regularly evaluate your time management abilities and make adjustments to guarantee that they continue to be successful in light of the changes that occur in both your professional and personal life. Experiment with a number of different methods, and then adjust your plan according to the one that yields the greatest results.

Utilizing these task prioritization and time management methods when working from home will help you successfully manage your workload, remain productive, and have a healthy work-life balance. Select the strategies that cater most closely to your needs and pursuits, and ensure that effective time management remains a central emphasis of your routine while you work remotely.

Setting boundaries between work and personal life

Because working remotely can make the line between work and personal life less clear, it can be challenging to strike and keep a good balance between work and other aspects of life. In this section, we'll discuss the importance of setting boundaries and provide some pointers on how to maintain separation between your professional and personal lives. We will go over how to set up a separate workstation, how to define work hours, and how to develop rituals that mark the beginning and finish of your workday, such as a pre-work routine or an after-work wind-down routine. In addition, we will go over how to create a work schedule that is realistic and attainable.

1. Setting up a separate workstation is one of the most successful ways for delineating the boundaries between one's home life and professional life. It is important to maintain separation between the areas in which you live and this room, which is to be used only for work-related activities. You may unconsciously associate your job with a certain location, which would make it easier for you to switch gears when you left that location.

2. When working from home, it is important to give yourself clearly defined work hours, just as you would if you were

working in a traditional office setting. It is possible that you may be expected to work a typical 9 to 5 schedule or to adjust your hours in order to accommodate personal duties such as attending childcare or getting regular exercise. Make sure that your coworkers, friends, and family are aware of your work hours so that they know when they may reach you and when they need to concentrate on their own tasks. This is important regardless of the schedule that you choose to follow.

3. Workday rituals. Developing rituals to signify the beginning and end of your workday will assist you in making a smoother transition between the time you spend working and the time you spend on your personal life. Some people have the habit of having coffee, reading the newspaper, or going for a walk before beginning their workday. In a similar vein, a routine for winding down after work may involve activities such as stretching, listening to music, or doing something enjoyable. These habits signal to your brain that it is time to shift gears, which makes it much easier to differentiate between your life at work and your life outside of work.

4. Establishing boundaries with others. It is important to communicate your boundaries with your family, friends, and coworkers so that they are aware of the times that you need to concentrate on your job and the times that you are available for personal connections. There are many different methods to do this, some of which include designating certain times of

the day as "quiet hours" at home, making use of visual cues such as a closed door or a sign that reads "do not disturb," and scheduling regular check-ins with your team in order to maintain connection while ensuring that your boundaries are respected.

5. When working remotely, it is essential to establish digital boundaries in order to maintain a healthy work-life balance. Examples of this include disabling email notifications outside of business hours, setting "away" or "do not disturb" statuses on various communication platforms, and even using separate electronic devices for work and personal use. By establishing clear digital limits for yourself, you may help avoid the temptation to constantly check your work email and attend to other job-related matters during your free time.

6. Prioritizing self-care and personal hobbies: if you want to prevent having your personal life be controlled by your professional duties, be sure to include time in your schedule for self-care and personal hobbies that take place outside of work hours. Make it a point to schedule time in your calendar for personal pursuits such as hobbies, physical activity, socializing, and leisure, and give these pursuits the same weight as your professional duties. If you put your own health first, you'll put yourself in a better position to strike a good balance between your professional and personal lives.

7. Conducting frequent analysis and alterations to boundaries. Because of the constant flux in both your personal and professional life, it is essential to conduct regular analysis and adjustments to your boundaries in order to guarantee that they continue to serve their intended purpose. Adjusting your work hours, rearranging your workspace, or coming up with innovative ways to communicate your boundaries with others are all examples of things that might fall under this category.

You may be able to have a healthy work-life balance even when working remotely if you implement these strategies for establishing clear boundaries between your professional and personal lives. Maintaining a wall of separation between your personal and professional lives can allow you to be more efficient and focused on work, while also allowing you to continue to have pleasure in your free time and ward against burnout.

Practice: examine your existing routine and find areas for improvement

This assignment is intended to help you analyze your current work-from-home habit and find areas where you might improve by applying the principles taught in this chapter. You will be able to reflect on your existing habits and design a specific action plan for establishing a more balanced and effective experience of working remotely by leading yourself through a self-assessment of your daily schedule, time management methods, and work-life boundaries. This will help you to create a detailed action plan for establishing a more balanced and productive remote working experience.

Step 1: analyze your typical day-to-day activities.

To get started, think about the way you normally go about your day. Take into consideration the following questions:

- How would you describe a typical day on the job for you?
- Is there anything that you do on a regular basis that you find to be particularly helpful or enjoyable?
- Is there anything about your routine that you find challenging or that doesn't work as well as it should?

Make a note of your comments, and then use them as a basis to identify aspects of your routine that could be improved.

Step 2: evaluate your current approaches to time management.

The next step is to evaluate the time management tactics you currently employ. Please take into consideration the following questions:

- How do you decide which tasks are most important and how to effectively organize your day?
- Do you put any effort into managing your time well, and if so, what strategies do you use, and if not, why not?
- Do you feel there are any aspects of your productivity or capacity to focus that may use some work?

Make a note of the responses you give, and if there are any problems or inefficiencies, come up with new strategies for managing your time.

Step 3: assess your current level of work-life balance.

Consider your current situation in terms of the work-life balance and then answer the following questions:

- How well do you manage to keep your personal and business life separate?
- Do you work in a designated workspace during regular business hours?
- Is there anything that happens in your personal life that spills over into your professional life and causes you stress or imbalance?

Create a list of your responses, and then think about ways in which you may improve the balance between your professional life and your personal life by setting or increasing limits.

Step 4: identify potential improvements.

On the basis of the information you gathered in steps 1 through 3, determine which aspects of your daily routine, methods of time management, and boundaries between work and personal life may need improvement. Create a list of these areas, and then consider the kinds of adjustments you may make to your approach in order to address the problems.

Step 5: create a personalized action plan.

To assist you in achieving a healthier and more productive work-from-home lifestyle, you should develop a personalized action plan that is based on the areas where you feel you need to improve. This strategy should include tasks or adaptations that you make to your daily routine, abilities in time management, and restrictions on the amount of work you do.

For instance, the following might be a part of your action plan:

• Establishing a reliable daily routine that includes fixed working hours and predetermined intervals for breaks

• Adopting a fresh method of time management, such as the Pomodoro approach or time blocking, and putting it into practice

• Establishing a fixed work area and establishing routines to denote the beginning and end of each workday are both important.

• Sharing your boundaries with your loved ones and your workplace is important.

Step 6: maintain a close watch on your progresses and make necessary alterations as you go.

Keep in mind that developing a profitable and useful habit for working from home will require consistent effort over time. Maintain consistent reporting and evaluation of progress and adjust your strategy to meet any changes that may be required. This may necessitate rethinking your daily routine, experimenting with new time management techniques, or looking for new ways to create a decent balance between your personal life and work commitments.

If you examine your current routine and look for ways to enhance it, you will be well on your way to building a more balanced and productive experience when working remotely. You will be able to save time if you do this. While you are working on implementing these changes, it is critical to remember to be patient and kind to yourself, as well as to recognize and honor your accomplishments along the way.

Chapter 4: Staying Active

Incorporating Physical Activity into Your Remote Workday

The importance of keeping a regular exercise and movement routine

Maintaining a physically active lifestyle is more important than ever in today's fast-paced atmosphere. The inclusion of regular movement and exercise into the daily routines of remote workers is critical to their overall health, mental well-being, and productivity. In this section, we will go more into the importance of physical activity for people who work from home. We will discuss the physical and mental health benefits of exercise, the impact that prolonged sitting has on health, and the role that physical activity has in managing stress and enhancing productivity.

The advantages of exercise for physical and mental health

Regular physical activity is widely acknowledged to provide numerous benefits to one's physical health, including the promotion of better cardiovascular health, the enhancement of both strength and flexibility, the facilitation of weight management, and the reduction of the risk of developing chronic illnesses. Furthermore, regular physical activity has been shown to have a significant impact on mental health. It can not only help to reduce stress, anxiety, and depression, but it can also enhance cognitive function, memory, and mood. By being active, remote workers may improve their general well-being and retain more energy, which can lead to increased productivity and a higher quality of life.

The harmful effects of prolonged sitting on one's health.

Working from home sometimes necessitates spending lengthy periods of time seated at a desk, which can be detrimental to one's physical health. Long durations of sitting have been linked to an increased risk of acquiring obesity, cardiovascular disease, diabetes, and some types of cancer. Sedentary behavior can also result in musculoskeletal imbalances, decreased flexibility, and poor posture, all of which can cause continuing pain and suffering. Employees who work from home may be inspired to make regular movement and exercise a priority in their daily routines after learning about the disadvantages of adopting a sedentary lifestyle.

Physical activity's contribution to stress reduction and productivity enhancement

Physical activity can boost both your capacity to deal with stress and your overall productivity. Endorphins are the body's natural feel-good chemicals, and exercise encourages the production of more of them, which can help relieve stress and promote sensations of serenity and relaxation. Furthermore, physical activity may provide a constructive outlet for venting the stresses and strains of one's job, which contributes to a more balanced mental state.

Furthermore, physical activity has been shown to boost cognitive function, increase attention and concentration, and inspire creative thinking. Employees who work from home can increase their productivity and problem-solving abilities by including physical activity into their working routines. This can eventually lead to greater professional success.

To summarize, making physical exercise a priority in one's routine when working remotely is critical to one's general health, mental well-being, and productivity. This contributes to general health. Though this remains true for us all, workers who are compelled to do their work from a remote place would be well to become acquainted with the numerous benefits that can be achieved from regular mobility and exercise. If they follow this advice, they will not only improve their physical and mental health, but they will also position themselves for long-term success in their employment.

A sedentary lifestyle can have a variety of negative consequences, some of which can be minimized by taking steps to break up long periods of sitting. Taking walks during breaks, stretching, and indulging in quick bursts of physical activity are some examples of such tactics. Remote workers may help themselves live a healthier and more balanced life by adopting daily routines that include time for both work obligations and exercise, as well as setting fitness goals that are both reachable and demanding.

This part will help you to include activity breaks into your daily routine.

A sedentary lifestyle may be bad for our overall health, but doing remote work typically requires sitting at a desk for long periods of time. To mitigate this, it is vital to add activity breaks into your workday, which may benefit both your physical and mental health. These rest periods should be taken on a regular basis. We'll look here at some practical techniques for incorporating fitness into your daily routine while working remotely. Setting reminders to take breaks, adopting standing or walking meetings, and taking quick exercise or stretching breaks to refresh and redirect your attention are some of these ideas. You will be able to maintain your productivity level throughout the day by adding regular exercise breaks, which will also benefit your overall health and well-being.

Set reminders for breaks.

Setting reminders for yourself at certain periods throughout the day may be an effective way to include exercise breaks into your working. These reminders may be set using a smartphone alarm app, a calendar software, or simply a conventional timer. You may train your brain to anticipate these breaks by forming a consistent pattern, making it easier to transition between times of intensive activity and periods of rest and rejuvenation. Taking regular breaks can help you prevent mental fatigue, enhance your productivity, and drive you to incorporate physical exercise into your daily routine.

Include meetings where people stand or walk around.

Meetings held while standing or walking are an excellent method to include fitness into your everyday work routine. Standing instead of sitting or using a treadmill desk can help you maintain a more active posture while participating in conference calls or other types of virtual meetings. Walking meetings, whether held outside or in the comfort of one's own home, may be an excellent technique to stimulate creativity, improve attention, and inspire better teamwork among team members. By including some type of physical exercise into daily meeting routine, you may not only enhance your personal health but also set a good example for your coworkers and help create a happier work environment.

Use your little pauses to exercise or stretch.

Taking a few minutes throughout your workday to conduct some mild stretching or exercise may be an effective approach to refocus your attention and recharge your batteries.

Consider allocating a few minutes every hour or two to physical exercise such as walking, stretching, or even a little bodyweight workout. These are all excellent choices. These breaks not only help to offset the negative consequences of sitting for a lengthy amount of time, but they may also provide a mental boost, allowing you to return to your job obligations with more focus and excitement.

Make use of technology to support your movements.

There are several software and mobile applications available to help you include movement into your everyday routine. For example, activity tracking apps and wearable devices may prompt you to get up and move about, count the number of steps you take each day, and even guide you through condensed versions of workout routines. It is much easier to keep your feeling of accountability and motivation when you utilize technology to create a more personalized and fascinating experience for yourself, making it much easier to follow an active lifestyle.

Create a supporting network.

It may be beneficial to connect with coworkers, friends, or family members that value an active lifestyle in order to obtain extra motivation and support. Incorporating fitness into your employment may be made more fun and gratifying if you tell others about your goals and progress toward them. This may promote a sense of belonging as well as accountability. The establishment of a support network may also be a great resource for the sharing of ideas, hints, and encouraging words among its members.

To recap, incorporating exercise breaks into your daily routine while working remotely may improve both your physical and mental health while also helping you to maintain a constant level of productivity throughout the day. Set reminders to take breaks, incorporate standing or walking meetings, utilize quick exercise or stretching breaks, leverage technology, and form a support network to create a more balanced and dynamic work environment that improves your overall well-being. All these tasks should be completed while at work.

Tips for staying motivated and creating an exercise routine.

Maintaining motivation and consistency is essential for getting the benefits of routine exercise when working remotely. To stay motivated and committed to your fitness goals, you must create an exercise regimen that meets your own needs and interests. This section will provide guidance on how to establish and keep up an exercise program that promotes your general health and wellbeing.

1. Set attainable fitness objectives. You can stay motivated and track your progress by setting reasonable and doable fitness objectives. Make sure your short-term objectives are

clear, quantifiable, and time-bound before anything else. You'll gain confidence and momentum as you accomplish these objectives, which can encourage you to stick with your fitness program. Progressively work toward longer-term objectives that are more difficult while making sure they are reasonable and compatible with your current level of fitness and way of life.

2. Discover activities you like. It can be simpler to maintain motivation and commitment to your workout regimen when you partake in physical activities you like. Try out several forms of exercise, such as walking, running, cycling, swimming, yoga, or strength training, to determine which you prefer and find most satisfying. Your workouts may stay fun and intriguing by mixing things up and attempting new things.

3. Make exercising a must-do in your daily schedule. Consider exercise to be as essential to your daily schedule as brushing your teeth or eating breakfast. The time of day that works best for you and is least likely to be interrupted is the time to schedule your workouts. You'll be more likely to adhere to your program and reach your fitness objectives if you prioritize exercise and make it a regular part of your daily schedule.

4. Utilize social network and support. You can maintain your motivation and dedication to your workout regimen by having a support structure and a sense of accountability. If you want

support and encouragement from others, talk to your friends, family, and coworkers about your fitness ambitions. You might also want to join a fitness organization or find a workout partner. Connecting with people who have similar fitness interests through social media and fitness apps can help with inspiration and accountability.

5. Divide the workout into smaller bits. If you find it difficult to find the time or the drive for longer workouts, think about splitting your fitness program up into smaller daily segments. Exercise sessions that are only a few minutes long, like quick walks or mini workouts, can be just as effective as longer workouts. Exercise might be easier to manage and incorporate into your daily routine if you break it up into smaller sessions.

6. Track your improvements. Monitoring your development can serve as a potent motivator, encouraging you to stick with your fitness program and appreciate the advancements you've achieved. To keep track of your workouts, use a fitness app, journal, or spreadsheet, noting the time, level of difficulty, and kind of activity you did. Regularly assessing your progress can give you a sense of success and keep you focused on your objectives.

7. Reward yourself. Rewarding yourself for your commitment and hard work is a great way to recognize your accomplishments and milestones. Rewards might be as straightforward as indulging in a favorite pleasure, treating

yourself, or investing in new exercise equipment. You'll reinforce the advantages of exercise and inspire yourself to keep working toward your fitness goals by recognizing your efforts and advancement.

In conclusion, it is crucial to maintain motivation and establish a consistent exercise schedule if you want to benefit from regular physical activity for your health, especially if you work from home. You'll be more prepared to establish and maintain an exercise routine that supports your general health and well-being if you set realistic goals, engage in enjoyable activities, make exercise a non-negotiable part of your daily schedule, use social support and accountability, break up exercise into smaller segments, track your progress, and treat yourself.

Practice: develop a daily movement plan and set fitness goals

We'll walk you through the process of developing a unique daily movement schedule and establishing fitness objectives in this workout. By taking the actions outlined here, you'll be better prepared to include exercise and mobility into your remote work schedule and meet your fitness objectives.

Step 1: assess your current activity levels.

Think back on your present levels of exercise to start. Think about how much time you spend each day standing, sitting, and exercising. Make a note of any areas that you'd want to see improved, such as lowering your time spent sitting down or increasing the time you spend working out.

Step 2: find movement opportunities.

Next, come up with ideas for including additional exercise in your everyday routine. Consider pursuits that fit easily into your remote work schedule, such as:

- Every hour, take a brief break to stretch or go for a stroll.
- Including meetings that are standing or walking.
- Practicing yoga or bodyweight workouts during lunch breaks.
- To run errands, use a bike or walk.

Step 3: create a daily movement plan.

Make a daily movement plan outlining when and how you'll fit in physical exercise using your list of movement possibilities. Make sure your plan is feasible and attainable given your present level of fitness, job schedule, and personal obligations by being explicit about the type and time of each exercise.

Your daily mobility schedule may, for instance, comprise the following:

- Prior to commencing work, a 10-minute stretching session.
- During the working days, two 15-minute walking breaks.
- A 30-minute exercise session during lunch.
- After work, go for a stroll or ride your bike.

Step 4: Create SMART fitness objectives.

The moment has come to create exercise goals that are consistent with your own goals for health and wellbeing now that you have a daily activity plan in place. When setting goals, follow the SMART (Specific, Measurable, Achievable, Relevant, and Time-Bound) principles:

- Specific: clearly state your goals (for example, "I want to run a 5K" as opposed to "I want to exercise more").

- Measurable: choose a method for keeping track of your progress, such as "I will run three times a week" or "I will increase my running distance by 10% each week."

- Achievable: make sure your objectives are reasonable and feasible considering your present level of fitness and the resources at your disposal (for example, choose "I will start by running one mile and gradually increase my distance" over "I will run a marathon next month").

- Relevant: pick goals that go hand in hand with your interests, values, and overall health goals (example: "I will run a 5K to improve my cardiovascular fitness and support a local charity").

- Time-bound: to help you stay motivated and focused, give yourself a deadline for completing your goal (for example, "I will run a 5K in three months").

Step 5: track your progress and make changes as necessary.

Review your daily movement schedule and fitness objectives frequently to gauge your progress and make any required modifications. Celebrate your victories and reached milestones and seize the chance to develop and learn from any difficulties. Maintaining flexibility in your strategy might help you stay engaged and motivated over the long run. Consistency is the key to success.

Finally, once you've finished this process, you'll have a clear plan for incorporating physical activity into your lifestyle of remote work and reaching your fitness objectives. To reap the rewards of an active and balanced remote work life, keep in mind to prioritize your health and wellbeing and to remain dedicated to your daily exercise plan and fitness objectives.

Chapter 5: Nutrition for Optimal Performance

Fueling Your Body and Mind

The Impact of nutrition on energy levels and cognitive function

Maintaining adequate energy levels and cognitive performance, both of which are important for remote workers, depends heavily on nutrition. In this part, we'll talk about the connection between nutrition and cognition with an emphasis on the value of eating a nutritious, well-balanced diet to promote mental clarity and productivity.

Carbohydrates, fats, and proteins make up the macronutrients.

Carbohydrates, lipids, and proteins, among other macronutrients, are essential for sustaining energy and maintaining cognitive function.

The body uses complex carbs as its main energy source, and whole grains, fruits, and vegetables are the best options for long-lasting energy. These carbs support steady blood sugar levels, avoiding energy dips and enhancing concentration.

Fats boost brain health and cognitive function, especially good unsaturated fats like those in avocados, nuts, seeds, and olive oil. Salmon and other fatty fish include omega-3 fatty acids, which are necessary for healthy brain function and have been linked to enhanced memory and focus.

Neurotransmitters, which are necessary for communication inside the brain, are constructed from proteins. Maintaining good cognitive function can be facilitated by consuming a range of protein sources, such as lean meats, fish, beans, and legumes.

Mineral and vitamin micronutrients

Vitamins and minerals are examples of micronutrients that are essential for maintaining general brain function. For instance, minerals like magnesium and zinc assist nerve function and the release of neurotransmitters, whilst B vitamins aid in the production of energy and the synthesis of neurotransmitters. Consuming a nutrient-dense diet full of fresh produce, whole grains, and lean protein sources will assist guarantee getting enough of these vital vitamins and minerals.

Hydration and cognitive function

Another important component of diet that has an impact on cognitive performance is hydration. Dehydration can cause weariness, attention problems, and a decrease in short-term memory. It's crucial to have enough water throughout the day to keep your mind at its best. Aim for at least 8 cups (64 ounces) of water each day; if you're physically active or in a warm area, you might want to drink more.

Remote employees may make educated nutritional decisions that improve their job performance and general well-being by knowing the effects of nutrition on energy levels and cognitive function. You can maintain brain health, attention, and productivity with a balanced, nutrient-dense diet and adequate water, guaranteeing that you can work well from home.

Tips for healthy meal planning and preparation

For remote workers who wish to maintain a nutrient-rich diet and promote optimal cognitive function, the ability to plan and prepare healthy meals is vital. The information we provide in this part will help you successfully plan and prepare meals, maintain your dietary objectives, and work toward achieving maximum productivity.

1. Make time for meal planning: schedule a certain period each week for making a grocery list and preparing your meals. This can help you save time, feel less stressed, and make sure you always have wholesome alternatives available.

2. Pick a variety of foods that are high in nutrients: your meal plan should include a variety of nutritious grains, lean meats, healthy fats, fruits, and vegetables. This type will provide you the nutrients you need for the best possible brain function and give you the energy you need all day.

3. Make a weekly food plan: include breakfast, lunch, supper, and snacks in your weekly meal plan. You'll be more organized, waste less food, and avoid making poor dinner decisions at the eleventh hour if you do this.

4. Use leftovers and cook in bulk to save time by preparing dishes in big quantities and reheating them for fast lunches or dinners. You can maintain portion control and prevent overeating with the aid of this strategy.

5. To make meal preparation during the week easier, prepare items in advance. Wash, cut, and store fruits and vegetables, or prepare grains and meats.

6. Use time-saving kitchen tools: to make meal preparation more effective and timesaving, use gadgets like slow cookers, Instant Pots, or air fryers.

7. Establish a schedule for meal preparation, such as cooking supper in the mornings before work or making the weeks' worth of lunches on Sunday evenings. You may develop a habit of eating well by following this practice.

8. Keep wholesome snacks on hand by stocking your pantry with whole-grain crackers, fresh fruit and vegetables, nuts, seeds, and other healthy snack options. Having these things on hand might help satisfy hunger and stop mindless munching on less healthy foods.

9. Be cautious of portion sizes: to prevent overeating, be attentive of portion proportions when preparing meals. You

may encourage healthy eating habits and maintain portion control by using smaller dishes and measuring out portions.

10. Plan for flexibility: because life may be erratic, it's critical to account for flexibility while making meal plans. For times when unplanned circumstances occur or when you're pressed for time, keep a few backup dinner suggestions on hand.

You may maintain a healthy diet that promotes optimum energy levels, cognitive function, and general well-being by adopting these suggestions and techniques into your routine for meal planning and preparation. Making healthy nutrition a priority as a remote worker may significantly improve your output and performance, enabling you to operate remotely at your peak capacity.

Strategies for avoiding common remote work dietary pitfalls.

The temptation to snack often, eat unhealthy convenience foods, or miss meals because of a busy work schedule are just a few of the nutritional issues that might arise from working remotely. We'll cover methods for avoiding these typical remote work dietary hazards and keeping up a regular healthy eating schedule in this subsection.

Establishing a regular meal schedule, setting up a separate dining area from your workstation, and filling your kitchen with wholesome snacks and meal components are some of these tactics. These techniques can help remote workers develop healthy eating habits and maintain a diet that is balanced and supports their general health, cognitive function, and energy levels.

1. Make a regular mealtime schedule: when working from home, it's important to establish a regular meal schedule, just like you would for a regular work schedule. The same time each day should be set aside for breakfast, lunch, and supper. If necessary, arrange breaks for snacks. You may prevent overeating or missing meals by being consistent, which will also help you keep your energy levels steady throughout the day.

2. Establish a separate eating area from your workspace to prevent multitasking or mindless snacking during meals. You'll be more inclined to pay attention to your food and use mindful eating techniques if you set up a particular place for dining.

3. Keep a variety of wholesome meal components and snacks on hand, including whole grains, lean proteins, fresh fruits, and vegetables. Stock your kitchen with nutrient-dense options. You'll be less likely to be tempted to grab for harmful convenience meals or takeout if you equip your kitchen with wholesome choices.

4. Prepare your meals and snacks in advance to assist you avoid making poor food choices when you're pressed for time

or feeling overburdened. For busy days, think about meal planning or keeping a list of quick, wholesome meal suggestions on hand.

5. Set limits on snacking: when working from home, it's simple to develop a habit of often snacking. Set times for snacks or only allow yourself to munch if you're hungry to prevent overeating.

6. Remain hydrated: to maintain energy levels and avoid overeating, you must consume enough water throughout the day. Keep a water bottle nearby to serve as a reminder to stay hydrated. You might also want to set hydration goals to make sure you're getting enough fluids. Always prioritize water over sodas.

7. Eat slowly and with awareness of your hunger and fullness cues so that your body has time to recognize when it is full. You may avoid overeating and have a better connection with food by engaging in mindful eating.

8. Give yourself permission to take pauses from work to enjoy your meals. Avoid working during meals. To avoid overeating or making bad food choices, avoid working or multitasking while eating.

9. Limit your access to harmful temptations by keeping them out of your house or out of sight. To avoid overindulging when you're desiring something sweet, think about portioning out just one dish.

10. Seek accountability and support: discuss your healthy eating objectives with family, friends, or coworkers to establish a support network and uphold accountability. To keep motivated and on track, think about signing up for an online group or taking part in a healthy eating challenge.

Remote workers may avoid typical nutritional errors and maintain a balanced diet that supports their energy levels, cognitive function, and general well-being by putting these guidelines into practice. Making healthy nutrition a priority when working from home may significantly improve your output and performance, enabling you to give your best work in a remote work environment.

Practice: write a weekly meal plan and assess your current eating patterns.

We'll walk you through the process of making a customized weekly meal plan and assessing their present eating patterns in this activity. A meal plan that combines a balance of macronutrients and micronutrients will be created to support their energy levels, cognitive function, and general health. This will include procedures for evaluating their current diet, identifying areas for improvement, and analyzing their food preferences.

Consider the following questions as you first think on your present eating patterns:

- Are you eating a varied diet that contains whole grains, lean meats, fruits, veggies, and healthy fats?
- Do you typically skip meals or snack excessively, or do you eat at regular times throughout the day?
- Do you frequently eat too much or choose unhealthy convenience meals out of boredom or stress?

Next, develop a weekly meal plan that includes a variety of nutrient-dense meals to support your energy levels, cognitive function, and general health using the information and advice in this chapter. To guarantee proper consumption of vitamins, minerals, and fiber, make sure to include a variety of fruits, vegetables, and whole grains in each meal, as well as a balance of carbs, fats, and proteins.

Consider the following suggestions when you make your food plan:

- Consider using seasonal produce in your meal plans because these items are frequently tastier, nutrient-dense, and affordable.
- To save time and avoid the temptation to rely on harmful convenience foods, batch prepare and portion meals in advance.
- Include a variety of wholesome snacks throughout the day to help control hunger and preserve energy levels, such as yogurt, fresh fruit, nuts, and almonds.

Finally, assess your new meal plan and contrast it with your past dietary practices. Recognize areas for development and resolve to make the required adjustments to produce a more healthy and balanced diet. As you make these adjustments, keep an eye on how your energy levels and cognitive function are affected. You can then tweak your meal plan as necessary to improve both your general wellbeing and productivity at work.

You should now be equipped with a clear roadmap for creating a healthy food plan that supports their energy levels, cognitive function, and general health while working remotely after completing this activity. Additionally, assessing and considering existing eating patterns can assist remote employees in identifying areas for development and implementing long-lasting adjustments that lead to a better lifestyle and improved job performance. Remember that establishing sustainable, healthy eating habits requires time and assistance since maintaining a balanced diet and placing a priority on nutrition is a process.

Section 3

Cultivating Mental and Emotional Well-being

Chapter 6: Mindfulness and Stress Reduction

Techniques for a Calmer, More Focused Workday

The benefits of mindfulness for remote workers

For remote workers, mindfulness has several benefits that can help them deal with the difficulties that come with working from home. The productivity, mental health, and stress levels of remote workers can all be improved by starting a mindfulness practice. We will examine the science of mindfulness in this section and talk about how it might assist remote workers in overcoming concerns including feelings of isolation, distractions, and issues with separating work and home life. Remote employees will be better able to incorporate mindfulness techniques into their daily routines and improve their general well-being and job performance if they are aware of its advantages.

1. Stress reduction: because of the ongoing connectedness, lack of boundaries, and blurred borders between work and personal life, remote work may be a substantial source of stress. By teaching the mind to concentrate on the here and

now and to cut back on negative thought patterns, mindfulness practice helps to alleviate stress. The better stress management skills of remote employees will result in better mental health and general wellbeing.

2. Better mental health: studies have shown that practicing mindfulness can lessen the signs of anxiety and despair. The mood-enhancing effects of mindfulness can help remote workers, who may feel more alone or disconnected. Remote workers can improve their sense of self-awareness and their ability to identify and deal with unpleasant emotions by engaging in mindfulness practices.

3. Productivity enhanced: mindfulness can aid remote employees in sharpening their attention and concentrating, which will enhance output. Remote employees may more effectively handle distractions, retain their concentration on projects, and finish work more quickly by training their minds to be present and attentive. Greater self-awareness, which mindfulness also promotes, can help remote workers spot and deal with any productivity barriers like perfectionism or procrastination.

4. Better work-life balance: mindfulness can aid remote employees in creating and upholding more sensible boundaries between their personal and professional lives. Remote workers may more easily switch between business and leisure pursuits by increasing their self-awareness and learning to be

completely present in each moment. This will help them maintain a better balance and prevent burnout.

5. Improved communication and cooperation: by encouraging more empathy and active listening, mindfulness can aid remote workers in building stronger communication and cooperation abilities. Remote workers may more successfully participate in group projects and comprehend their coworkers' viewpoints by being completely present during virtual meetings and dialogues.

6. Increased resilience: remote employees who practice mindfulness are more able to adjust to change and deal with setbacks. Remote workers can more successfully negotiate the difficulties that come with working from home, such as technology problems or shifting deadlines, and recover more rapidly from setbacks by fostering an attitude of acceptance and non-judgment.

Understanding the advantages of mindfulness can help remote workers better appreciate how these practices can promote their well-being and improve their productivity. Remote workers can benefit from gains in productivity, work-life balance, resilience, communication, and stress reduction by adopting mindfulness into their daily routines. This will ultimately result in higher job satisfaction and general well-being.

Incorporating mindfulness into your daily routine

The complete spectrum of advantages that mindfulness has to offer, including less stress, improved mental health, and increased productivity, can be experienced by remote workers by incorporating mindfulness practices into their daily routines. In this part, we'll provide you some pointers and techniques for adopting mindfulness into your routine so that it becomes a reliable habit that benefits both your mental and emotional health and productivity at work.

1. Set up devoted time each day for meditation or other mindfulness practices: setting out certain hours each day for meditation or other mindfulness practices is one of the most efficient methods to incorporate mindfulness into your everyday routine. Make sure to stick to it, whether it's meditating for 10–20 minutes every morning or taking quick mindful breaks all throughout the day. Try to commit to a regimen that works for you and your schedule since consistency is important.

2. Include mindfulness in daily activities: mindfulness is a skill that can be developed in a variety of contexts outside of formal meditation sessions. Find ways to incorporate mindfulness into your daily activities, such as eating meals slowly, focusing on your breathing while you walk, or participating completely in conversations with friends and family. You may create better awareness and presence in

many areas of your life by applying mindfulness to routine tasks.

3. Utilize technology to aid your practice: using technology to aid your mindfulness practice can be very beneficial. Numerous apps that offer guided meditations, mindfulness exercises, and progress tracking are available for mindfulness and meditation. Calm, Insight Timer, and Headspace are a few of the well-liked choices. You may also set calendar alerts or reminders to remind you to meditate or take mindful breaks throughout the day. You can design a customized mindfulness practice that suits your requirements and interests by utilizing technology.

4. Make your workspace a mindful space: how well you can practice mindfulness at work can vary greatly. Think about adding things that encourage focus and relaxation to your workstation, such plants, peaceful colors, or relaxing background noises. Eliminate pointless interruptions and clutter and create a special area for quick mindfulness or meditation breaks. You can more readily incorporate these practices into your everyday routine by setting up a workspace that encourages mindfulness.

5. Practice mindfulness while working: mindfulness can be especially helpful when performing focused and attention-demanding duties at the office. Try single tasking, which is giving one activity your whole concentration at a time, or the

Pomodoro Technique, which entails working in focused intervals and taking quick pauses. Both strategies can help you practice mindfulness while working. You may increase your productivity and overall job satisfaction by applying awareness to your work responsibilities.

6. Practice mindful movement: including mindful movement in your daily routine, such as yoga, tai chi, or even stretching, can enhance your general wellbeing and help you maintain a strong mind-body connection. These procedures may be especially helpful for remote employees who may spend a lot of time sitting at a desk. Make time each day for mindful movement and think about signing up for online courses or using how-to videos to help you with your practice.

By incorporating mindfulness into their daily routines, remote workers can establish a dependable mindfulness practice that promotes their mental and emotional well-being and increases their productivity. Through dedicated meditation sessions, mindfulness during daily activities, technology use, setting up a mindful workspace, incorporating mindfulness into work tasks, and practicing mindful movement, remote workers can take advantage of the full range of benefits of mindfulness. In the long run, this will improve general wellbeing and job satisfaction.

Practice: develop a daily mindfulness practice and track its impact

In this activity, we'll show you how to design a daily mindfulness practice that fits your requirements and preferences. You may use these techniques to create a tailored mindfulness practice that enhances your mental and emotional well-being and increases your productivity at work.

Step 1: select mindfulness techniques.

Start by investigating several mindfulness practices to see which ones speak to you. Several well-liked strategies include:

- Mindful breathing: pay attention to how your breath feels as it enters and leaves your body.
- Body scan: visualize your entire body, from head to toe, and note any tightness or feelings.
- Loving-kindness meditation: develop sentiments of love and compassion for both you and other people.

Pick one or more methods to add to your regular mindfulness practice.

Step 2: set a regular practice schedule.

Make mindfulness meditation a regular part of your schedule. Select the time of day that is best for you to practice, such as right when you wake up, during a lunch break, or right before bed. Try to practice for 10 to 20 minutes each day, or more if you prefer.

Step 3: create a dedicated space for mindfulness.

Set aside a location in your house or place of employment for your mindfulness practice. This area needs to be peaceful, cozy, and distraction-free. You could want to include components that encourage relaxation, such a cozy couch or chair, delicate lighting, or soothing artwork.

Step 4: begin your daily mindfulness practice.

Start your daily mindfulness practice by setting up your preferred methods, timetable, and environment. Keep in mind that developing mindfulness is a skill that needs time and persistence as you practice. Be kind to yourself and endeavor to treat your ideas and feelings without rebuke.

Step 5: track the impact of your mindfulness practice

Track the effects of your mindfulness practice on your stress levels, concentration, and general well-being to determine its efficacy and make any modifications. You might want to keep track of your observations in a notebook, spreadsheet, or app. Some things to take into account when tracking are:

• Stress levels: keep track of any variations in your stress levels before and after engaging in mindfulness exercises.

• Productivity and focus: check to see whether your mindfulness practice affects your capacity for concentration and task completion.

• Emotional health: consider any alterations in your general attitude and emotional condition following the start of your mindfulness practice.

Step 6: make adjustments to your practice

Based on what you've learned, make any changes to your awareness habit that you think are necessary. This can mean trying new things, shortening your practice times, or changing the way you exercise. Keep in mind that your mindfulness practice should be able to adapt to your changing needs and tastes.

After you finish this task, you will have a customized mindfulness practice with the skills and techniques you need to support your mental and emotional health and do a better job at work. As you keep practicing awareness, you might find that it becomes a natural part of your daily life, making you more resilient, able to focus, and happy in general.

Online Resources

1. Mindful.org (https://www.mindful.org/): a comprehensive website with articles, guided meditations, and practical tips for cultivating mindfulness.

2. Headspace (https://www.headspace.com/): a popular mindfulness app offering guided meditations, articles, and courses for various aspects of life, including stress reduction, focus, and sleep.

3. Insight Timer (https://insighttimer.com/): A meditation app featuring thousands of guided meditations, music tracks, and talks from mindfulness experts.

Mindfulness schools and trainings

1. Mindfulness-Based Stress Reduction (MBSR) (https://www.umassmed.edu/cfm/mindfulness-based-programs/mbsr-courses/about-mbsr/): an 8-week course developed by Jon Kabat-Zinn, PhD, at the University of Massachusetts Medical School. MBSR is widely recognized as an effective program for reducing stress and enhancing well-being.

2. Mindful Schools (https://www.mindfulschools.org/): offers online courses and resources for educators, parents, and professionals interested in integrating mindfulness into their work with children and adolescents.

3. The Mindfulness Training Institute (https://www.mindfulnesstraininginstitute.com/): provides a range of mindfulness-based courses, workshops, and teacher training programs led by experienced mindfulness instructors.

4. The Oxford Mindfulness Centre (https://www.oxfordmindfulness.org/): affiliated with the University of Oxford, this organization offers online and

in-person mindfulness courses, workshops, and teacher training programs.

5. The European Associations for Mindfulness (EAMBA) (https://www.eamba.net/): EAMBA offers mindfulness-based courses and teacher training programs, including Mindfulness-Based Stress Reduction (MBSR) and Mindfulness-Based Cognitive Therapy (MBCT). The institute offers training in various European countries.

6. The Mindfulness Academy of Belgium (https://www.brusselsmindfulness.be/): located in Brussels, the Brussels Mindfulness offers a range of mindfulness courses, workshops, and teacher training programs in English and Dutch. They focus on MBSR, MBCT, and other mindfulness-based approaches to support well-being and mental health.

7. The Centre for Mindfulness Research and Practice (CMRP) (https://www.bangor.ac.uk/mindfulness/): affiliated with Bangor University in Wales, CMRP offers a range of mindfulness courses, workshops, and teacher training programs, including MBSR and MBCT. They also conduct research in the field of mindfulness and its applications.

8. The Institute for Mindfulness-Based Approaches (IMA) (https://www.institute-for-mindfulness.org/): located in Germany, IMA offers comprehensive mindfulness training,

including MBSR, MBCT, and Mindfulness-Based Compassionate Living (MBCL) programs. They provide courses and teacher training programs in various European countries, with some courses available in English.

9. The Institut Français Pleine Conscience Mindfulness (https://pleineconscience-mindfulness.fr/): Located in France, the IFPCM offers mindfulness training programs, workshops, and courses, including Mindfulness-Based Stress Reduction (MBSR), Mindfulness-Based Cognitive Therapy (MBCT), and other mindfulness-based interventions. They provide programs for individuals, professionals, and organizations in French. The IFPCM also offers teacher training programs for those who wish to become certified mindfulness instructors.

These resources and mindfulness schools can provide readers with additional support and guidance as they develop their mindfulness practice.

Chapter 7: Dealing with Loneliness and Fostering Connections

Social Strategies for Remote Workers

The importance of social connections for well-being and productivity

A fundamental human need, social interactions offer emotional support, a sense of community, and chances for both personal and professional development. Strong social ties are crucial for remote workers to sustain their motivation, mental health, and overall job happiness. We will look into the value of social connections for remote employees in this section, as well as the difficulties they have while fostering relationships in a virtual setting.

1. Social support and stress reduction: remote workers can manage stress more successfully if they have a solid network of relationships that they can lean on. Social assistance can offer support, counsel, and a sympathetic ear during trying times, assisting in reducing the detrimental effects of stress on mental health and general wellbeing.

2. Resilience and adaptability: having strong social ties can help people be more resilient and adaptable, which makes it easier for remote workers to deal with challenges and changes. A supportive network can offer insightful advice, helpful tools, and other support to help people adjust to and succeed in their remote work environment.

3. Enhanced workplace performance might result from coworkers feeling connected to one another and supportive of one another. Remote workers are more likely to be motivated, engaged, and committed to their work when they feel like they are a part of a supportive team, which leads to improved productivity and job satisfaction.

4. Mental health and general well-being: research has revealed that social relationships have a big impact on both mental health and general well-being. Strong relationships with friends, family, and coworkers are more likely to result in remote employees feeling less anxious, depressed, and lonely, which improves their quality of life.

5. Feeling of community and belonging: working remotely can occasionally cause emotions of loneliness and alienation. Making and sustaining social ties can help remote workers feel a part of a community and a sense of belonging, which can make working from home more enjoyable and gratifying.

6. Possibilities for personal and professional growth: strong social links might present possibilities for personal and

professional growth for remote workers. It is possible for remote workers to enhance their careers by networking within their field, taking part in online communities, and forming mentoring relationships.

Despite the many advantages of social connections, remote workers frequently encounter difficulties in building relationships because there is less opportunity for informal socializing and face-to-face interaction. To reap the full spectrum of advantages that social connections can provide, remote workers may need to be more deliberate about building relationships and giving social activities top priority.

Remote employees should emphasize establishing and maintaining relationships as a crucial part of their work-life balance by being aware of the importance of social connections for wellbeing and productivity. By putting the techniques and exercises covered in this chapter into practice, remote workers may create a solid, encouraging network that improves their motivation, mental health, and level of job satisfaction, which will ultimately result in a more fruitful and satisfying remote work experience.

Strategies for building and maintaining relationships while working remotely.

Being purposeful and trying to maintain relationships when working remotely is necessary for general wellbeing and productivity. This section will go through numerous methods that remote employees can use to maintain relationships with coworkers, acquaintances, and family members despite being geographically separated.

1. Regular virtual check-ins: arrange frequent voice or video chats with family, friends, and coworkers to preserve relationships and stay informed about each other's life. These check-ins can make up for the absence of impromptu face-to-face conversations that would ordinarily take place in a conventional workplace setting or social context.

2. Utilize communication tools: to stay in touch with your network, communicate updates, and have casual discussions, utilize instant messaging, collaboration platforms, and social media. By facilitating more regular and varied communication, these tools can make it simpler to preserve relationships despite physical distances.

3. Create online social gatherings: to promote relationships with your distant coworkers and friends, organize online gatherings like virtual coffee breaks, game nights, or movie nights. These gatherings can assist recreate the casual social interactions that are frequently absent from remote work environments, strengthening team relationships.

4. Attend virtual conferences, webinars, or workshops to meet like-minded experts and build your network within your field. In your sector, networking can help you discover new

opportunities, remain current on trends, and build connections with possible mentors or partners.

5. Join online forums, discussion groups, or social media groups connected to your interests or field to meet people who are passionate about the same things you are. These groups can help you connect with new people who share your work concerns and aspirations while also offering helpful tools, ideas, and support.

6. Place a higher priority on in-person interactions: to preserve and deepen your relationships, plan in-person get-togethers with friends, family, and coworkers whenever you can. When it is safe and practical to do so, try to prioritize these connections. Even sporadic face-to-face meetings can have a big impact on the quality of your relationships.

7. Express thankfulness and encouragement to your friends, family, and coworkers in order to build supportive relationships and deepen your relationships. By expressing gratitude for their work and talents, you can contribute to creating a pleasant environment that encourages loyalty, trust, and understanding.

Remote workers can overcome the challenges of building and maintaining relationships in a virtual environment by proactively putting these strategies into practice. They will then benefit from having strong social links for their welfare and productivity. Physical distance can be addressed through regular, deliberate interaction and communication, allowing remote workers to maintain a strong network of allies that promotes their overall performance and enjoyment.

Virtual team-building activities and events

The development of relationships between distant coworkers and the development of a sense of community within a distributed team can be greatly aided by virtual team-building activities and events. This section will examine numerous virtual team-building exercises that might boost remote workers' motivation, engagement, and sense of community.

1. Online icebreakers: to help team members connect on a more personal level, begin virtual meetings with entertaining icebreaker questions or games. These icebreakers can inspire team members to open up and reveal more about themselves, fostering closer bonds and greater understanding between coworkers.

2. Set aside time for regular virtual team lunches so that everyone on the team may dine together and chat informally. This shared social hour can serve to mimic the casual conversations that take place in a conventional office setting and provide team members a chance to interact personally.

3. Remote team challenges: to promote cooperation and teamwork, set up friendly competitions like trivia contests, virtual escape dungeons, or creative tasks. These exercises

can promote teamwork and friendly competition while also aiding team members in improving their problem-solving and communication abilities.

4. Organize for team members to participate in online seminars or training sessions together to promote learning and collaboration. Team members can develop professionally together and are inspired to assist one another's growth through these shared experiences.

5. Host virtual brainstorming meetings for the team so they may work together on projects, exchange ideas, and come up with solutions. These meetings can encourage team members to collaborate more successfully by fostering a sense of shared ownership over initiatives and projects.

6. Celebrate successes and milestones: send virtual congratulations or acknowledgements to team members on their achievements, as well as to mark work anniversaries or personal milestones. You can contribute to the development of a supportive and upbeat team culture by expressing gratitude for the efforts and accomplishments of team members.

7. Retreats for virtual teams: plan a getaway for virtual teams that combines workshops, planned activities, and casual socializing. Team members may have the chance to develop stronger bonds, think back on their collaboration, and develop a common vision for the future as a result.

8. Regular one-on-one or team-wide check-ins and feedback sessions should be scheduled to examine team dynamics, resolve any issues, and pinpoint areas for development. These discussions may contribute to the development of a team environment that values open communication, trust, and cooperation.

9. Cross-functional teams and collaborative projects: encourage team members to collaborate on these endeavors or to form such teams. Employees may be able to connect with coworkers from various areas as a result, increasing their viewpoints and encouraging a sense of cohesion within the company.

10. Virtual volunteer options: arrange for team members to take part in community service projects or virtual volunteer opportunities. Through these activities, team members can strengthen their bonds and further a greater cause.

Remote workers can strengthen relationships with their coworkers, foster a sense of belonging within the team, and increase overall team cohesiveness and productivity by adding these virtual team-building activities and events into their daily work routine. Remote teams can overcome the obstacles posed by distance by prioritizing team building and keeping a focus on forging connections, as well as by establishing a good, encouraging work atmosphere that enables everyone to thrive.

Practice: assess your current social connections and create a plan for improvement

We will now walk you through the process of evaluating your current social relationships and identifying areas for development in this exercise. We'll provide a step-by-step process for assessing the quality and variety of your interactions, both inside and outside of the workplace. We will also provide advice on how to put together a strategy that incorporates the tactics covered in this chapter in order to strengthen and preserve social ties.

Remote employees will have a clearer awareness of their present social network after completing this activity, as well as a strategy for cultivating relationships that will enhance their productivity and well-being.

Step 1: evaluate your present social network.

Make a list of all your current social ties, including friends, family, and coworkers. Think back on how often and how well you interacted with each person. Think about whether these connections give you the encouragement, support, and feeling of community you require to succeed in a remote work setting.

Step 2: determine what needs to be improved.

Look over your list and mark any areas where you believe your social connections could be more diverse or strong. You might observe, for instance, that most of your interactions with coworkers are task-focused or that you don't have many relationships with people outside of your immediate team. Additionally, you might notice that since you started working remotely, certain relationships have grown tense or distant.

Step 3: establish concrete objectives for improving your social connections.

Determine precise objectives for enhancing your social ties based on your assessment. Increasing the frequency of encounters with select people, improving the depth of your chats, or growing your network of connections are a few examples of this. When describing your objectives and the methods you intend to use to achieve them, be realistic and detailed.

Step 4: create a plan for improvement.

Decide for improving your social connections using the techniques covered in this chapter. This could entail setting up virtual check-ins with loved ones on a regular basis, planning team-building exercises online, or joining online groups for your interests or area of work. Prioritize activities that are in line with your personal and professional goals while considering the many tools and platforms that are available to promote communication and collaboration.

Step 5: carry out your strategy.

By combining the techniques and routines you've identified into your everyday routine, you can put your strategy into action. Be patient and persistent in your efforts since developing and maintaining connections requires time and work. To make sure you're moving forward with your goals, periodically assess your progress and make any plan adjustments.

Step 6: evaluate your performance and revise your strategy as necessary.

Regularly evaluate your success as you carry out your plan and make any required revisions. Think about if your methods are working to help you achieve your goals and whether they are still relevant and realistic. Be willing to attempt new tactics or change your goals to better fit your current needs and priorities if you discover that some activities or approaches aren't functioning as well as you'd intended.

You will have a clearer awareness of your present social network after completing this exercise, as well as a strategy for cultivating relationships that will promote your wellbeing and productivity. Maintain a deliberate focus on cultivating your connections over time and continue to prioritize relationship-building since solid social ties are essential to your overall success as a remote worker.

Chapter 8: Preventing Burnout

Recognizing Warning Signs and Implementing Self-Care Practices

Understanding the signs and causes of burnout.

Burnout is a condition of prolonged physical and emotional tiredness that is frequently felt by remote workers for a variety of reasons. The causes and symptoms of burnout will be covered in this section, making it easier for remote employees to spot the warning signals and take preventative action. Remote employees can maintain their health and productivity by being able to recognize the causes of burnout.

Common signs of burnout include:

1. Even after a full night's sleep, feeling constantly exhausted and drained may be an indication of burnout. Your concentration and ability to do your work efficiently may be hampered by this tiredness.

2. Irritability: when burnout sets in, there may be an increase in irritability and mood swings. You might notice that you easily lose patience with minor difficulties or become irritated with coworkers.

3. Reduced productivity: as you fight to stay focused and motivated, burnout can cause a decline in work performance. You might discover that duties take longer to finish or that you can't provide the same outcomes as previously.

4. Disengagement: when you're burned out, you could feel cut off from your coworkers and job, losing interest in your duties and obligations. This may lead to a lower sense of accomplishment and job satisfaction.

5. Physical symptoms: physical signs of burnout include headaches, muscle tension, and digestive problems. Your capacity to perform at your best may be further impacted by these symptoms.

6. Long-term burnout can lead to mental health problems like anxiety and sadness, which can have a negative effect on your general well-being.

Factors that predispose remote workers to burnout:

1. High workload: remote workers may encounter high workloads as a result of heightened expectations or a failure to distinguish between work and personal life. Long hours and a lot of stress may result from this.

2. Lack of control over work: remote workers may feel as though they have less influence over their working conditions, which can cause them to feel frustrated and helpless. Communication issues and a lack of rapid assistance from coworkers or superiors may make this situation worse.

3. Insufficient praise: working remotely can make it more challenging to get credit for your efforts and feedback. Feelings of exhaustion may be exacerbated by this lack of appreciation.

4. Poor work-life balance: due to the blurring of the lines separating work and personal life, remote employees may find it difficult to maintain a healthy work-life balance. This may result in overworking yourself and skipping self-care routines.

5. Social isolation: working remotely can cause emotions of loneliness and seclusion, which can add to burnout. Remote workers may feel alienated and separated from their work without consistent social engagement and support from coworkers.

6. High levels of stress: due to variables including workload, lack of control, and isolation, remote workers may face higher levels of stress. Burnout and general well-being can both be negatively impacted by persistent stress.

Remote employees may address these issues and maintain their wellbeing and productivity by being aware of the symptoms and causes of burnout. To avoid burnout and ensure a sustainable remote work experience, it is important to promote a healthy work-life balance, practice self-care, and seek help from coworkers and managers.

Tips for maintaining a healthy workload and managing stress.

We will offer advice and techniques in this section to help remote employees keep a balanced workload, control their stress levels, and lower their risk of burnout. These procedures can help remote workers maintain a healthier work-life balance and safeguard their general wellbeing.

1. Achievable goals and priorities should be set, and overcommitting to work or projects should be avoided. Be honest with your team or supervisor about the amount of work you can complete in a certain amount of time.

2. Time management strategies: to organize your workday and maintain focus on your duties, utilize time management techniques like the Pomodoro Technique or time blocking. These methods can assist you in setting aside enough time for each work and avoiding feelings of overwhelm.

3. When it is feasible, assign assignments to coworkers or team members in order to distribute the effort and keep it manageable. This encourages teamwork and collaboration within your team while also assisting you in managing your personal stress.

4. Setting boundaries: to avoid overworking and maintain balance, set clear boundaries between work and personal life, such as set work hours and a distinct workplace. Maintain

these boundaries with yourself and people around you to prevent work-related stress from affecting your personal life.

5. Schedule regular pauses throughout the day to allow yourself to rest, recharge, and avoid burnout. Take a break from your work, partake in a stress-relieving activity, or just go for a stroll to rest and reenergize.

6. Using transparent communication: discuss your workload, expectations, and any issues you're encountering with your team and supervisors to make sure you're on the same page and get the help you need. Unambiguous communication helps reduce confusion and work-related stress.

7. Making self-care a priority: include self-care activities in your daily routine to support your physical and emotional health, such as regular exercise, a healthy diet, and enough sleep. You'll be better able to manage stress and keep up a healthy workload if you take care of yourself.

8. Making self-care a priority: include self-care activities, such as regular exercise, a balanced diet, and enough sleep, in your daily routine to support your physical and mental wellbeing. If you look after yourself, you'll be better equipped to handle stress and maintain a healthy workload.

9. Using techniques to reduce stress. Use stress-reduction techniques like meditation, deep breathing exercises, or progressive muscle relaxation. Regularly applying these

techniques can help you manage stress better and protect your mental wellbeing.

10. Asking for help from superiors and coworkers: if you need help, ask your superiors and coworkers. They may be able to offer suggestions, resources, or even just a sympathetic ear to help you manage your stress and maintain a manageable workload.

Remote employees can effectively maintain a healthy workload, manage stress, and lower their risk of burnout by putting these recommendations and tactics into practice. Their general well-being will be supported and their ability to thrive in their remote work environment will be made possible by this proactive approach to work-life balance.

Self-Care strategies for remote workers

We will now look at a variety of self-care techniques that remote workers can use to promote their wellbeing and avoid burnout. Remote employees can preserve their mental and emotional health and sustain their productivity over time by prioritizing self-care.

1. Regular physical activity: take regular pauses during the day to walk around or exercise to increase energy, lower stress, and improve general health. Make time each day to engage in activities you enjoy, such as strength training, yoga, or walking.

2. Nutritionally sound eating: give your body and mind the fuel they need with wholesome meals and snacks to help you operate at your peak. To enhance your cognitive performance and general wellbeing, prepare your meals in advance, remain hydrated, and steer clear of processed foods.

3. Get enough sleep every night to boost your mood, your ability to think clearly, and your general well-being. To enhance the quality of your sleep, create a sleeping-friendly environment, establish a regular bedtime ritual, and reduce screen time before bed.

4. Practice mindfulness to better manage stress and increase focus. Examples of mindfulness practices include meditation and deep breathing exercises. You will be more prepared to tackle the difficulties of remote work if you regularly practice mindfulness.

5. Social connections: to promote a sense of community and support, maintain and cultivate relationships with friends, family, and coworkers. To build your social network, schedule frequent virtual check-ins, engage in online communities, and give face-to-face encounters priority whenever you can.

6. Making time for interests and hobbies: to stay energized and retain a sense of balance, schedule time for interests and hobbies you find enjoyable outside of work. The pursuit of

personal interests can boost happiness and well-being by giving you a constructive outlet for stress.

7. Whenever necessary, seeking professional assistance. For assistance with stress management and wellbeing maintenance, speak with a therapist, counselor, or coach. Professional assistance can provide insightful advice and practical coping mechanisms for overcoming the difficulties of remote work.

8. Setting boundaries: to avoid overworking and maintain a healthy balance, clearly create and explain boundaries between work and personal life. This may entail establishing strict working hours, designating a specific workstation, and conveying your boundaries to family members and coworkers.

9. Developing a daily thankfulness practice involves thinking about the facets of your life and job that you value. This routine can assist you in turning your attention away from stress and difficulties and toward the positive facets of your life, resulting in a more balanced viewpoint.

10. Schedule brief pauses during your job to allow yourself to rest and refuel. Take use of this time to rest and unwind by doing things like reading, going for a stroll, or briefly practicing mindfulness.

11. Putting self-compassion and relaxation first: schedule time each day for self-compassion and relaxation. This can involve relaxing activities, such taking a warm bath or practicing

progressive muscle relaxation, as well as treating oneself tenderly and sympathetically when things are difficult.

Remote workers may support their mental and emotional health, avoid burnout, and sustain their productivity over time by putting these self-care techniques into practice. Self-care can be prioritized by remote workers to build a more fulfilling and long-lasting remote work environment.

Practice: identify your personal burnout warning signs and develop a self-care plan.

We will walk you through the process of identifying your own potential burnout warning signals and creating a unique self-care strategy in this activity. Remote employees will have a clearer awareness of their burnout risk factors after completing this activity, as well as a strategy to promote their wellbeing and preserve their productivity.

Step 1: consider previous experiences.

Consider any instances in the past where you may have felt drained or overburdened. Describe the sensations you felt at those times, such as exhaustion, impatience, a lack of motivation, or a sense of helplessness. As your own personal burnout warning signs, note these symptoms.

Step 2: determine your triggers.

Take into account the elements that led to your previous burnout. These could be overworked employees, a poor work-life balance, a lack of social support, or high-stress environments. Make a list of the things that make you feel burned out to better comprehend the conditions that can cause burnout.

Step 3: evaluate the circumstance you're in now.

Think about how things are right now in your life and at work. Do you have any burnout triggers right now? Do you currently exhibit any of your burnout symptoms? Be truthful with yourself about your current state of health and the dangers of burnout.

Step 4: create a self-care strategy.

Make a personalized self-care plan that considers the warning signals and causes of your burnout. As a starting point, think about the self-care techniques covered previously in this chapter as well as the following:

a. Physical self-care: include regular exercise, a balanced diet, and enough sleep in your daily schedule to promote your general health and wellbeing.

b. Engage in mindfulness exercises, develop an attitude of gratitude, and engage in self-compassion exercises to maintain emotional balance and manage stress.

c. Prioritize establishing and sustaining social ties with friends, family, and coworkers in order to provide a sense of community and support.

d. Take care of your intellectual well-being by scheduling time for hobbies and endeavors that stimulate and engage your mind, such as reading, picking up a new skill, or indulging in creative activities.

e. Maintain a healthy workload and avoid burnout by setting realistic goals, using good time management, setting boundaries, and communicating with your team.

Step 5: carry out your self-care strategy.

Implement your self-care strategy by making these habits a part of your daily routine. Make self-care commitments that are non-negotiable by scheduling time for these activities. Keep in mind that self-care is essential for preserving your wellbeing and productivity.

Step 6: follow your development.

Check in with yourself frequently to evaluate your wellbeing and the success of your self-care strategy. Be flexible in your approach and patient with yourself as you create new habits. Maintaining self-awareness and being willing to adapt when necessary are crucial.

Step 7: ask for help if you need it.

If you discover that your self-care strategy is insufficient to stop burnout or deal with your warning signals, think about getting expert assistance from a therapist, counselor, or coach. These experts can offer direction, advice, and resources for stress management and wellbeing upkeep.

Remote employees will have a greater awareness of their own personal burnout warning signals after completing this 7 steps review, as well as a practical plan to prioritize self-care, prevent burnout, and preserve their wellbeing and productivity. Keep in mind that self-care is a continuous activity that calls for constant dedication and attention. Maintaining a proactive self-care routine will help you manage the difficulties of working remotely and keep up a rewarding, long-lasting job.

Section 4

Personal and Professional Growth

Chapter 9: Developing a Personal Growth Plan

Enhancing Your Career and Life Satisfaction

The process of creating a personal growth plan to improve your work and life satisfaction will be covered in this chapter. You may advance your remote job by identifying areas for both personal and professional growth and creating attainable goals. We'll offer advice on how to maintain accountability and motivation throughout your growth process so that you reach your full potential. A personal growth plan can act as a roadmap to help you reach your goals, whether you are looking to advance in your current position, change careers, or simply enhance your general wellbeing.

Identifying areas for personal and professional development

As remote workers, it is necessary for us to continue our personal and professional development in order to adapt to the ever-changing terrain of the working world and create a career that is meaningful. You will have a much better idea of the actions you need to take in order to get the results you want if you first identify the areas in which you might use improvement. The following advice will assist you in determining areas in which you could improve as well as charting a course toward better success and satisfaction:

1. The first step in conducting an effective self-assessment is to take stock of your existing knowledge, capabilities, and areas for improvement. Think about the aspects of your life in which you thrive and those in which you may stand to improve. If you want to acquire insight into your professional qualities and areas in which you may improve, you might want to think about using self-assessment tools such as personality tests or skills inventories.

2. Seek feedback: try to solicit the opinions of your coworkers, superiors, or mentors regarding the areas in which you excel and those in which you may need more work. They might supply useful insights and make suggestions for advancement that you hadn't thought of before that they bring to your attention.

3. Find out what you want to accomplish: consider both your long-term professional goals and your overall life goals. What prior knowledge or experiences will be necessary for you to accomplish these objectives? You will be able to customize your expansion strategy to meet your goals if you first determine what outcomes you are looking for.

4. Conduct research on the current state of the market and make it a habit to keep abreast of the most recent innovations and trends in your industry. You will be able to identify prospective growth areas that can boost your knowledge and marketability if you stay current with new skills, technology, and best practices by keeping up with fresh information.

5. Determine which areas of personal and professional growth are most important to you and rank them in order of importance, taking into account the resources you have at your disposal and the goals you have set for yourself. Put your attention on the things that will have the most bearing on the success of both your work and your life overall.

You may construct a clear vision for both your personal and professional development by doing an assessment of the talents you now possess, soliciting feedback from others, and giving thought to your long-term goals. This will serve as a basis for you to set objectives that are attainable and develop a plan to fulfill your full potential in the field that you are pursuing while working remotely.

Setting achievable goals and tracking progress

The key to keeping your motivation up and assuring your success on your journey of personal and professional development is to set goals that you can achieve and track your progress toward achieving those goals. The following techniques are ones that can assist you in establishing objectives that are attainable, slicing those objectives into smaller, more manageable chunks, and keeping tabs on your progress along the way:

1. Use the SMART criteria: when you set your goals, make sure they are Specific, Measurable, Achievable, Relevant, and Time-bound. Using these criteria will help you achieve success. This framework assists you in establishing targets that are not only clear and attainable but also capable of being monitored and evaluated successfully.

2. Convert more ambitious objectives into more manageable steps: your main objectives should be broken down into a series of smaller, more attainable tasks or milestones. As a result, it will be much simpler for you to concentrate and remain motivated, as you will be able to rejoice in even the most insignificant of your accomplishments along the way.

3. Rank order your goals in order of importance: organize your objectives in order of relevance and speed of completion. Your focus should be on those that are most closely aligned with your long-term goals and will have the most impact on the satisfaction you derive from both your profession and your life.

4. Create a timeline: create a timeline outlining how you intend to achieve your goals, including specific dates by which each activity or milestone must be finished. Remember to

keep things in perspective and allow for little wiggle room in case there are any surprises along the way.

5. Create a tracking system: to keep track of your work and ensure that everything is in its place, create a tracking system using a tool such as a diary, spreadsheet, or software for managing projects. Maintain regular updates to your tracking system to ensure it accurately reflects completed work, and make necessary alterations to your timeframe.

6. Create a schedule of regular check-ins: set up a schedule for yourself to meet with you periodically so that you may evaluate your progress and make any required alterations to your plan. This might help you maintain accountability and ensure that you are continuing to move forward in the direction of your goals.

7. Seek support and make yourself accountable: tell a reliable friend, member of your family, or a mentor about your plans so that they can encourage you and keep you accountable to following through with your strategy. Maintaining your motivation and being focused on your growth journey can be aided by maintaining regular check-ins with your support network.

8. Recognize and honor your accomplishments, no matter how minor they may seem, and enjoy the milestones you've reached along the way. Your motivation can be boosted and your dedication to your own personal and professional

development can be strengthened when you acknowledge the progress you've made.

9. Continuously evaluate on your progress and take into consideration any barriers or challenges you've run into, and then alter your strategy accordingly. Make use of this new information to change your plan and hone your objectives as required to ensure that they continue to be applicable and within your reach.

10. Keep a growth mindset, which means you should view obstacles, such as failures, setbacks, and challenges, as opportunities for learning and development. Develop a "growth mindset" by perceiving your skills as malleable and acknowledging that you can improve your performance through the application of effort and perseverance.

You will be able to set objectives that are attainable, track your progress, and keep the momentum going in your journey toward personal and professional improvement if you put these tactics into action. As a result, you will be able to consistently enhance your skills, competence, and resilience, which will, in the end, improve the satisfaction you derive from your career and life as a remote worker.

Tips for staying motivated and accountable.

The pursuit of one's own professional and personal growth necessitates complete focus, perseverance, and continuous self-discipline. The ten ideas listed below can help you stay motivated and hold yourself accountable as you work toward attaining your growth objectives:

1. Create a compelling vision: the first step in developing a compelling vision is to create a sense for your ideal future that is both vivid and motivating. This vision should include both your personal and professional goals. Imagine yourself already successful on a regular basis and draw motivation from this mental image.

2. Establish more manageable and intermediate objectives: divide your long-term objectives into more manageable and attainable stages. This enables you to celebrate your progress toward smaller goals and keep the momentum going while you work toward achieving your overall goals.

3. Keep a growth mindset, which means you should view obstacles, such as challenges and failures, as learning and development opportunities. Develop a "growth mindset" by perceiving your skills as nimble and acknowledging that you can improve your performance through the application of effort and perseverance.

4. Establish a daily routine that supports your growth goals by adopting habits and practices that are in alignment with your aims. Create a routine by following these steps. The key to success is consistency, as even seemingly insignificant advances can build up to significant gains over time.

5. Surround yourself with people who will encourage and inspire you. Create a support system consisting of people who share your growth mindset, such as friends, family, mentors, and peers. These people should be able to provide you with encouragement, advice, and accountability.

6. Find a guide or a tutor: seek the advice of a mentor or coach who specializes in the same areas of development as you do and has experience in those areas. They can offer insightful advice, constructive criticism, and supportive assistance, all of which can assist you in staying on track and overcoming obstacles.

7. Participate in a mastermind group or professional community: take part in a mastermind group or professional community where you may share your objectives, challenges, and triumphs with other people who have a similar outlook on life. This important support might assist you in maintaining your motivation and holding yourself accountable.

8. Keep an eye on how far you've come and adjust as necessary: evaluate how far you've come toward achieving your objectives on a regular basis and make any adjustments. This will assist you in maintaining your focus on your goals, gaining insight from any failures, and refining your strategy for growth.

9. Make use of digital tools and applications: make use of digital tools and applications to assist you in remaining

organized, tracking your progress, and staying accountable. To help you along your path to personal development, you might find it helpful to use a habit tracker, an app that helps you manage projects, or a goal-setting tool.

10. Reward yourself for accomplishments: whether they are big or small, you should celebrate your successes by treating yourself with something special or going on an adventure just for you. This might help you remain committed to your personal growth journey and provide the drive you need to keep working toward achieving your goals.

Keeping yourself motivated and accountable while working toward your personal and professional development objectives is possible if you put these suggestions into practice. As a remote worker, making a concerted effort like this will make it possible for you to continually expand your skills, expertise, and resilience, which will, in the end, improve the satisfaction you derive from both your career and your life.

Practice: create a personal growth plan with specific goals and milestones

To make a thorough personal growth plan that will direct both your personal and professional development, follow these steps:

Step 1: consider your present position.

Take some time to assess your present situation, both personally and professionally. Think on your accomplishments, areas for development, and any recent feedback from coworkers, managers, or mentors. Choose the areas of your life or profession that you want to develop or improve.

Step 2: define your growth areas.

Make a list of specific growth areas to concentrate on after taking reflection time. These could consist of:

- Gaining fresh knowledge or abilities
- Enhancing one's capacity for leadership or communication
- Improving your well-being or work-life balance
- Building your network of professionals
- Aiming for a promotion or changing careers

Step 3: establish SMART objectives: specific, measurable, achievable, relevant, and time-bound.

Create SMART objectives that spell out your aims for each area of improvement. Your objectives should be:

- **Specific**: clearly state the goal you intend to achieve.
- **Measurable**: include measurements that can be used to gauge your progress.
- **Achievable**: check that the objective may be attained given your current resources and limitations.
- **Relevant**: match your objectives to your larger personal and professional ambitions.

• **Time-bound**: establish a target date for completing your task.

Step 4: divide objectives into more manageable milestones.

Break down each of your objectives into more compact, reachable milestones. These milestones will act as steppingstones toward your bigger goals, letting you monitor your development and keep your motivation high.

Step 5: create a progress timeline.

Make a schedule for completing your objectives and milestones. This could be as straightforward as a calendar or Gantt chart, or it could be a list of target dates. Make sure your schedule is reasonable and doable in light of other obligations and responsibilities.

Step 6: locate resources and assistance

Make a list of the tools and assistance you'll need to accomplish your objectives. This could incorporate:

• Books, training sessions, or curriculums

• Networks of professionals, coaches, or mentors

• Time, effort, and money are all resources.

Step 7: create systems for accountability

Plan for how you'll hold yourself accountable for your advancement. Several possibilities are:

• Sharing your objectives with a peer, mentor, or close friend

• Joining a professional organization or mastermind group

- Using applications or digital tools to monitor your progress

Step 8: review and modify your plan on a regular basis.

Set-up regular check-ins to evaluate your progress, acknowledge your successes, and make any required changes to your strategy. You'll be able to stay on course, learn from any setbacks, and streamline your growth process by doing this.

You will have developed a thorough personal growth plan based on your objectives and aspirations after finishing this task. You may confidently begin your growth journey with this roadmap in hand since you will have a clear path to higher success and job happiness in your remote setting.

Chapter 10: Networking and Advancement in a Remote World

Strategies for Staying Connected and Visible

The value of networking and career progression in a remote work environment will be covered in this chapter. To ensure career growth and development as a remote worker, it is crucial to be engaged and visible within your company and sector. We'll offer pointers for productive virtual networking and relationship-building, as well as methods for keeping your name in the public eye and remaining in touch with your coworkers and superiors. You may enhance your career and expand your professional network while working remotely by using these techniques.

The importance of networking for career growth

We'll talk here about the value of networking for remote employees and how it helps with professional advancement. Building and sustaining connections with people in your business or sector through networking may result in new possibilities, partnerships, and career progress. Networking can be extremely important for remote employees for a number of reasons:

1. Maintaining visibility: since working remotely may reduce your visibility to coworkers and superiors, it's critical to actively network and keep relationships. You may increase your prospects of job progression by being connected and visible, which will help to guarantee that your effort is acknowledged and respected.

2. Access to opportunities: through networking, you may find out about work opportunities, projects, and other possibilities inside your company or sector that you would not otherwise be aware of. You will improve your chances of finding new employment prospects and receiving recommendations from your contacts by growing your network.

3. Knowledge exchange: networking enables you to share ideas, insights, and industry best practices with others, which promotes innovation and professional development. You may expand your knowledge and help your industry grow by getting in touch with others who have similar interests and areas of expertise.

4. Creating a professional reputation: as you network and form connections, you may create a name for yourself in your company or sector as a resource with knowledge and professionalism. A robust professional reputation might result in more chances, visibility, and credibility.

5. Support and mentorship: networking can put you in touch with peers, mentors, or collaborators who can offer career-long support, encouragement, and direction. You may overcome obstacles, learn new skills, and receive insightful information that will advance your career with the aid of these relationships.

6. Creating a community: by giving remote workers a sense of community and belonging, networking can also assist to lessen feelings of loneliness and detachment. You may create a support network that enhances your general well-being and level of job satisfaction by interacting with people who have similar experiences to your own.

Tips for effective virtual networking and relationship-building

As a remote worker, there are a number of networking and relationship-building tactics you may use to develop your career. If you work from home, you may not have access to the same kinds of possibilities for face-to-face networking that people who do their jobs in conventional office settings do. Despite this, there are still a plethora of opportunities to develop your network and build relationships in a virtual setting. Below we offer advice on how to effectively create relationships and participate in virtual networking:

1. Take the initiative to get in touch with coworkers, superiors, and other experts working in your industry. Be proactive in this endeavor. Do not sit around waiting for other people to take the initiative. When you show real interest in other people and the work that they do, you can develop connections that will last.

2. Leverage social media: to connect with other professionals in your field, make use of social media platforms such as LinkedIn, Twitter, and Facebook. Join groups that are particular to your sector, take part in the conversations that are held there, and offer content that is pertinent in order to demonstrate your expertise and communicate with others.

3. Participate in virtual events, such as webinars, virtual conferences, and online networking events, in order to expand your professional network and get fresh knowledge on developments in your sector. Be sure to keep in touch with any new connections you make at these events and continue the conversation.

4. When engaging in professional networking, it is imperative that you remain genuine and authentic in all your interactions. Exhibit interest in other people and their work, and don't be afraid to be candid about your own experiences and the difficulties you've faced. Authenticity is a factor in the development of trust, which in turn helps to enhance relationships.

5. Give something of value; networking should always result in a win-win situation for both parties. Give something of value to the people you're connected to by sharing insights, resources, or opportunities with them that they might find interesting. This helps to position you as a useful contact, and it also has the potential to lead to better partnerships.

6. Maintain consistent communication: make sure you regularly check in with your contacts, provide them with updates, and share content that is pertinent to your network. Both the relationship and the demonstration of your continued dedication to your network are strengthened as a result of this.

7. Use tools for virtual collaboration such as video conferencing, instant messaging, and software for managing projects in order to collaborate and communicate with coworkers and other experts. Even if you are working remotely, these tools can assist you in maintaining connections and establishing new ones.

8. Personalize your outreach: when reaching out to new contacts, make sure you take the time to research their history and hobbies before sending them a message so that you may tailor it to their specific needs. This implies that you are genuinely interested, and it may lead to deeper and more significant connections.

9. Developing a powerful professional network is a time-consuming endeavor that requires you to exercise patience and

perseverance. Be patient and keep in mind that building relationships is a long-term investment in the development of your profession. If you are steadfast in your efforts, you will eventually come to appreciate the fruits of your investments.

10. Seek out possibilities for mentorship and coaching. Look for instances in which you may either receive mentoring from more seasoned professionals or provide mentoring to individuals working in your industry. This can contribute to your personal professional growth and development while also assisting you in the establishment of solid relationships with others.

If you put these suggestions into action, you will be able to effectively network and create relationships while working remotely, which will help you stay connected, visible, and positioned for career advancement. If you make the most of the chances that virtual networking offers, you'll discover that working remotely doesn't have to mean sacrificing a strong sense of connection or the ability to work together effectively.

Strategies for staying visible and connected within your organization.

The tactics for being visible and connected within your business as a remote worker are covered in this part. You may keep a strong presence within your organization and continue to progress in your career by actively engaging in team meetings, working on projects, and showcasing your worth and experience. Following are some tips for keeping active and connected:

1. Regular communication: use email, instant messaging, or video conferencing to stay in touch with your team members and managers. Update them on your assignments and initiatives, solicit their opinions, and keep them informed of your progress.

2. Attend virtual team meetings: try to join virtual team meetings and group discussions. Participate actively in these sessions. Ask questions, express your thoughts, and show that you are interested in the team's aims and objectives.

3. Work together on projects: look for chances to work together on projects with your coworkers, either by contributing your knowledge or by actively looking for collaborative initiatives. By doing so, you'll be able to demonstrate your abilities and create closer relationships with your team members.

4. Share your successes: frequently let your team and superiors know about your triumphs. This might assist show how valuable you are to the company and serve as a reminder of your contributions.

5. Offer help and encouragement: be proactive in extending your assistance and knowledge to coworkers. You may improve your connections and develop a reputation as a

dependable, informed professional by being a helpful and productive team member.

6. Seek feedback and possibilities for development: request comments on your work from your managers and coworkers and look for chances to advance professionally within the company. This indicates your dedication to development and constant improvement.

7. Participate in business culture and events: attend company-wide events like online social gatherings, team-building exercises, or training sessions. This will show your commitment to the culture and principles of the company and help you maintain contact with your coworkers.

You can keep a strong presence in your company and grow your career ambitions by putting these methods in motion.

Practice: develop a networking plan and identify key contacts to reach out to

In this exercise, we will walk you through the process of creating a networking plan and selecting critical people in your professional network for you to contact. You can stay connected, increase your network, and enhance your remote career by developing a methodical approach to networking. To create your networking strategy, follow these steps:

1. Define your networking goals: begin by defining your networking objectives, such as seeking new career prospects,

growing your expertise in a specialized field, or developing contacts with professionals in your business.

2. Determine key contacts: make a list of people in your current network who can assist you in achieving your networking goals. Colleagues, bosses, previous coworkers, and industry experts may be included. Identify prospective new contacts, such as professionals in your sector, alumni from your institution, or participants in industry events or forums, to connect with.

3. Do some research on your connections before you get in touch with them. Find out about their history, present position, and hobbies. This will enable you to customize your outreach and create a deep relationship.

4. Make your outreach plan: create a strategy for communicating with your contacts that specifies the channel (email, phone, social media, etc.), the timing, and the goal of your outreach. Be explicit in your request and provide something of value in exchange, such as knowledge sharing, advice, or useful resources.

5. Plan follow-ups: after contacting your contacts, plan frequent follow-ups to keep the connection going and to keep the relationship growing. Be considerate of their time and make sure your follow-ups are worthwhile and pertinent.

6. Attend virtual networking events: look for webinars, conferences, and virtual networking events in your sector to

meet new people and learn about opportunities and trends in your area.

7. Follow your development: keep a log of your networking efforts, including the people you've contacted, the results of your interactions, and any further steps. Keep track of your progress and modify your networking strategy as you see fit.

You will have a better networking strategy after finishing this exercise that will enable you to grow your professional network, maintain touch with important connections, and progress your remote career.

Putting It All Together

Chapter 11: Creating Your Customized Wellness Blueprint

A Holistic Approach to Thriving in Your Remote Career

Reviewing key takeaways from each chapter

In the course of this guide for remote workers, we have discussed a wide variety of subjects with the goal of assisting them in achieving professional success and fulfillment in their jobs. In this section, we will provide a comprehensive picture of the tactics and insights required to do more than survive in a remote work environment by summarizing the most important lessons from each section of the book.

1. Embrace the revolution of the remote workplace. It is vital, in order to adjust to this new world of work, to understand both the benefits and the challenges of working remotely. Develop essential abilities such as efficient communication, time management, and self-discipline, and you will increase your chances of succeeding in a remote workplace. Creating clear goals, routines, and keeping open lines of communication with your team will help make the transition to working remotely go as smoothly as possible.

2. Create a home office that is both practical and motivating to work in. Make sure that your home office is one that allows you to be productive, comfortable, and motivated. Ensure that your workspace has appropriate ergonomics, select a suitable location with a low level of distractions, and customize the area with things that motivate you. Maintaining a productive atmosphere at work requires doing regular assessments of your working space and implementing any necessary changes.

3. Create habits that are good for your health. Create a daily routine and schedule that you can stick to in order to integrate your work and personal life more successfully. Establish clear boundaries between your work and your personal life, and learn to prioritize duties utilizing time management approaches. You may avoid risks of burnout and make improvements to your general well-being if you create and stick to habits that are good for your health.

4. Maintain your activity level and put healthy nutrition first. Movement and exercise on a consistent basis are essential for both one's physical and mental wellbeing. Make moving breaks a regular part of your workday and come up with an exercise regimen that takes into account both your preferences and the constraints of your schedule. Make nutrition a top priority by organizing and preparing nutritious meals and snacks, and steer clear of the typical nutritional hazards that come with remote work.

5. Fostering your mental and emotional health should be a priority. Mindfulness activities have been shown to be effective at lowering stress levels and improving focus, both of which can contribute to a calmer and more productive workday. While you are working remotely, incorporating mindfulness practices into your day-to-day routine and exploring strategies to combat loneliness and foster social connections are both important things to do. Take part in virtual team-building activities to improve your sense of belonging and deepen your relationships with coworkers.

6. Take care of yourself and avoid getting burned out. Recognize the warning signs and factors that contribute to burnout, and then take action to prevent unhealthy workloads and effectively deal with stress. Create a self-care plan that incorporates pursuits that will help you relax, get your energy back, and advance your own personal development. You may protect your mental and emotional health by making self-care a top priority, which will increase the likelihood that you will be successful in your remote endeavors on the long run.

7. Create a strategy for your own personal development. Determine areas in which you might improve personally and professionally to increase the enjoyment you get from your work and your life. Establish goals that are within your reach, keep track of your progress, and maintain your motivation by recognizing even the little victories and getting support from

more experienced individuals or from peers. Review your growth plan on a regular basis in order to keep the momentum going and to drive continual improvement.

8. Network and advance in a remote world. Even in a setting in which one works alone, cultivating professional relationships is essential for career advancement. Create successful techniques for virtual networking, ensure that your presence is known throughout the organization, and cultivate relationships with fellow workers and industry leaders. You can gain access to new opportunities and develop in your remote profession if you keep connected to others and maintain a public profile.

In conclusion, if you want to be successful in a remote working environment, you need to take a holistic approach to your personal growth and your professional development. You may build a solid foundation for future success by participating in the growing trend of remote work, designing an inspirational workspace for yourself at home, establishing healthy routines, and placing a high priority on your mental and emotional wellness. In addition, continuing one's own personal development while also expanding one's professional network is necessary for professional advancement.

Remote employees have the opportunity to create a well-rounded and satisfying career if they put the ideas and insights presented in this guide into practice. In order to keep moving forward and continue developing in your career, it is important to remember to periodically analyze your progress, to hold yourself accountable, and to change your strategy as necessary.

Integrating the advice and practices into a cohesive wellness plan

With this recap of the most important lessons from this guide fresh in mind, it's time to start putting together a comprehensive health strategy using the recommendations we have highlighted. You may develop an all-encompassing strategy for prospering in your remote employment if you focus on improving every component of your well-being self. As you design your blueprint for wellness, take into consideration the following steps:

1. Assess your current situation: think about the habits you now have at work, the routines you follow, and your overall health. Determine the areas in which you shine and those in which you may pour some effort. Your wellness plan will benefit greatly from the firm foundation provided by this self and genuine assessment.

2. Establish concrete objectives: using the results of your self-evaluation, establish concrete objectives that are attainable and relate to each facet of your overall well-being. These objectives ought to be attainable, quantifiable, and time-

bound; in this way, you'll be able to monitor your progress and modify your strategy as required.

3. Plan for each of your goals: for each of the goals that you have set for yourself, devise a detailed plan that outlines the actions that you will take in order to accomplish them. Establish a schedule for the implementation of the plan, and take into consideration any resources or support that you might require.

4. Establish priorities: find out which of your objectives and plans are the most important to your health, and then rank order them from the most important down. You should make sure that you leave time in your daily and weekly schedule to concentrate on these goals, as this will ensure that you stay consistent and devoted to your fitness strategy.

5. Keep an eye on how far you've come: assess how far you've come toward achieving your objectives on a regular basis and adapt your approach accordingly. Honor your victories and take the time to reflect on and gain wisdom from any failures or difficulties you may have experienced along the way.

6. Monitor your accountability: to assist you in maintaining your accountability to your wellness plan, make use of the tools, services, and support networks available to you. This could entail recruiting a coach or an accountability partner, taking part in a mastermind group, or making use of various digital tools to monitor your development.

7. Stay nimble: as your needs and circumstances change, maintain a flexible attitude toward your wellness plan in order to maintain its relevance and effectiveness. Maintaining alignment with your personal and professional development requires that you regularly evaluate your goals and tactics and make any necessary updates.

You may construct a comprehensive wellness blueprint that is suited to your one-of-a-kind requirements and goals if you take a holistic approach to your health and incorporate the guidance and activities detailed in each chapter. This plan will serve as a roadmap for you to follow while you pursue a career that allows you to work remotely, assisting you in achieving better levels of success, satisfaction, and general well-being.

Tips for staying accountable and maintaining progress.

Consistency, motivation, and responsibility are necessary to carry out your health plan and make long-term adjustments to your work and lifestyle. Here are some pointers to assist you in maintaining momentum and staying on par as you work to fulfill the objectives included in your wellness blueprint:

1. Set definite, specific, and measurable objectives. Setting specific goals will help you stay focused and on track. Achieving defined, quantifiable, and time-bound goals will

make it simpler to monitor your progress and decide whether you are headed in the correct direction. Instead of choosing a general objective like "improve my work-life balance," choose something more specific like "limit work-related tasks to 45 hours per week and dedicate at least two hours per day to personal interests."

2. Organize your objectives into manageable steps. Large goals can occasionally feel overwhelming, which makes it challenging to stay motivated and on track. To get around this, divide up your goals into smaller, easier-to-achieve activities or phases. With this strategy, your objectives will seem more attainable, and the satisfaction you will feel as you complete each step will keep you motivated. For instance, if your objective is to establish a regular exercise schedule, start by determining the kinds of physical activities you enjoy, looking up appropriate workouts or classes, and planning a few quick training sessions each week. Increase your workouts' frequency and duration gradually as you get more fit and more self-assured.

3. Plan frequent check-ins. Staying accountable and making any necessary changes to your wellness blueprint depend on regular evaluation of your progress. Plan regular check-ins with yourself to review your progress toward your goals, such as monthly or quarterly assessments and write it down. Think about what is going well, what challenges you are

encountering, and what adjustments you might need to make to keep on course during these check-ins. Documenting your progress will help you gain useful insights into your patterns, routines, and potential areas for development. Never be reluctant to change your strategy and attempt new tactics if you realize that some objectives or tactics are not yielding the desired results. Your wellness blueprint should be flexible and adaptable to your changing demands because its main goal is to promote your growth and well-being.

4. Enlist assistance. Sharing your wellness plan with a close friend, relative, or mentor helps increase accountability and drive. Select a companion who is compassionate, understanding, and genuinely concerned about your well-being. They can assist you in staying on track while you work toward your objectives by providing inspiration, direction, and helpful criticism. Think about scheduling frequent check-ins with your accountability partner so you can go through your accomplishments, issues, and development. You may find it easier to stay motivated with this collaborative method because you'll know that someone else is rooting for your success.

5. Enjoy your success. Maintaining drive and self-confidence requires acknowledging and enjoying all your accomplishments, no matter how minor. As you complete sections of your wellness blueprint, stop to evaluate your

progress and give yourself a treat. Celebrations might be as straightforward as indulging in a tiny treat, taking the day off, or telling your accountability partner about your accomplishments.

Your positive habits and behaviors that contribute to your overall success are reinforced when you acknowledge and appreciate your accomplishments. In turn, this promotes resilience in the face of setbacks or difficulties and aids in the development of a growth mentality.

In conclusion, it takes explicit goal setting, breaking down objectives into small chunks, periodically monitoring your progress, mobilizing assistance, and celebrating your successes in order to stay accountable and continue progress in your remote work journey. You may build a rewarding and successful remote career while putting your health first by implementing these suggestions and your wellness blueprint.

Create your own well-being blueprint, taking insight from each chapter, and establish clear deadlines for execution and review.

Now that you have learned important lessons from each chapter, it is time to put what you have learned into action by creating a thorough health plan that is specific to your requirements as a remote worker. This plan will operate as a road map for enhancing your success, contentment, and general well-being when working remotely.

1. Start by identifying your needs. consider the most important lessons from each chapter and decide which parts of your well-being need the greatest work. Your work environment, work-life balance, physical activity, diet, mental and emotional health, personal development, and networking opportunities might all be considered.

2. Establish clear objectives and benchmarks. create SMART (specific, measurable, attainable, relevant, and time-bound) objectives for each facet of your wellbeing. These objectives ought to be unique to your requirements, preferences, and situation. Choose the checkpoints or milestones that will enable you to monitor your progress and assess your success.

3. Create a progress and accountability plan. Make a strategy for keeping responsibility and tracking your progress if you want your wellness blueprint to be successful. This may be planning frequent check-ins with yourself, asking a dependable friend or mentor for advice, or utilizing productivity and health apps to monitor your routines and accomplishments.

4. Implement your wellness blueprint. It's time to begin putting the ideas and behaviors you have selected into action now that your entire wellness plan is in place. Be kind to yourself and understand that it takes effort and time to make

permanent changes. Be ready to encounter obstacles as you strive toward your objectives and keep in mind that they are normal facets of the maturation process.

5. Regular check-ins and adjustments should be made. It's crucial to constantly review your wellness blueprint as you advance in your remote work journey and make any required improvements. You can stay on track with these check-ins, spot any areas that need improvement, and modify your strategy as your requirements and situation change. To make sure your health plan stays applicable and useful, think about setting up regular or quarterly evaluations.

6. Adopt a growth mindset. With a growth mindset, embark on your remote work adventure with the understanding that there is always space for progress and that difficulties present chances for learning and growth. Be willing to give new tactics and methods a try, and always look for ways to improve your general well-being and remote work experience.

7. Celebrate your success. Remember to recognize your accomplishments, no matter how modest, as you strive toward your wellness objectives. Recognizing your accomplishments and praising yourself for your efforts helps keep you motivated, increase your self-esteem, and promote the good habits and actions that are essential to your success.

Finally, developing a thorough wellness blueprint is a crucial first step to finding long-term success and fulfillment in your remote career. You may create a meaningful and sustainable remote work lifestyle that promotes your physical, mental, emotional, and professional growth by adopting a holistic strategy that addresses all facets of your well-being.

Remember to always be kind to yourself while you carry out your personal health plan and recognize your accomplishments along the way. You can overcome the difficulties of remote work and take advantage of the fantastic opportunities it presents if you are determined, responsible, and have the correct methods in place. We wish you well and plenty of success as you embark on your enhanced remote work journey!